EXPLORING ENGLISH

5

Tim Harris, illustrated by Allan Rowe

Teacher's Manual

Introduction by

Jean Zukowski/Faust

 **LONGMAN**

Exploring English 5: Teacher's Manual

Addison Wesley Longman, 10 Bank Street, White Plains, NY 10606

Editorial Director: Joanne Dresner
Acquisitions Editor: Anne Boynton-Trigg
Production Editor: Liza Pleva
Text design: Curt Belshe
Text design adaptation: PC&F, Inc.
Cover design: Curt Belshe

ISBN 0-201-83396-4

1 2 3 4 5 6 7 8 9 10-CRS-02 01 00 99 98 97

Contents

Preface

Welcome to *Exploring English!* You will find here, in this fifth book of the six-book series, a context-rich setting for learning English. Featuring a broad variety of presentations and based on the development of a cast of memorable characters, *Exploring English* will set your students on the road to English-language fluency quickly and easily. Communicative student-centered activities enable students to engage in meaningful communication from the first day of class. A wealth of exciting activities for individuals, pairs, and groups is integrated into a careful and logical sequence of grammar concepts, functions, themes, and lifeskills to enable learning in an enjoyable and motivating classroom setting.

This complete course presents a balanced combination of the four skills:

Listening is practiced through teacher presentation of Conversations and Readings, and through the use of the audiocassette tapes. Practice in active listening is provided through the illustrated situations and accompanying stories in the section *What's Happening Here?*

Speaking is practiced through repetition of Conversations, by imitating the taped segments, by doing the Pair Work exercises, by responding to in-class invitations to communication such as the Free Response and One Step Further activities, and by answering the questions in the exercises.

Reading is practiced as the student follows the taped presentations, reads along with the teacher, does individual preparation for Pair Work exercises, strives to understand the directions, and relates to and recognizes the concepts that are depicted in the illustrations.

Writing is practiced from the beginning in the Written Exercises that are part of the carefully planned progression and interweaving of skills in the text. Students can also be encouraged to copy sections of the text and to combine elements in the text to expand on their naturally growing ability in English. They can also be encouraged to write out the exercises, filling in the blanks with newly learned and carefully cued items.

The text offers a great deal for a teacher to work with. The illustrations will often remind students of experiences of their own. Encourage your students to talk about these experiences in English as they explore their own worlds through the medium of the English language.

Good teaching involves the students in the real use of the language; hence, *Exploring English* is full of naturally generated opportunities for natural verbal interaction on topics of interest to students because the topics are relevant to their lives and necessary for them to learn. Students will eagerly do oral practice of the kinds that are found in the text because the topics relate to them in a clear context.

ABOUT THE STUDENT BOOK

The Student Book (*Exploring English 5*) has eight units. Chapters 4 and 8 are Review chapters. Within each unit there are several sections, although the units are not so formalized as to be totally predictable.

Typically, a chapter opens with illustrated Conversations. Each of these Conversations is presented on an audiotape as well as in the text. By using the audiotape, the teacher can provide an alternative presentation of the material in a different voice. The audiotape can also be viewed as advantageous from another perspective: The material is presented through one medium only—listening—a practice that gradually lessens student dependence on the teacher and increases the student's ability to understand language without other supporting clues, such as facial expressions, gestures, or the written word.

Each Conversation is likely to serve as a springboard for a Pair Work exercise in which the students practice the newly presented elements.

New words are taught in New Vocabulary sections as well as in other parts of the chapters. Additional new vocabulary is taught within Conversations and even within exercises. The new words and concepts are presented in contexts—in ways that illustrate the concepts and give students useful sentences. The teacher can act out some words, point to some words as they are pictured in the illustrations, and use realia to both present and reinforce the new words. Practice exercises are provided to reinforce the pronunciation and recognition of these words. It is important to note that new words are introduced gradually; the heaviest concentration of new words in each chapter is generally found in the What's Happening Here? section, a reading with one or more illustrations that have been planned to demonstrate the meanings of new material.

Grammar Treatment

In *Exploring English,* all new grammar is presented as a natural extension of the preceding elements. The teacher will find no clinical grammar explanations, as each new grammatical element is presented in a carefully controlled context so that it will be totally comprehensible. In addition, each grammatical form is both reinforced and reviewed in clearly illustrated formats such as cartoon stories, dialogue stories, and regular prose stories.

New structures are presented in heavily contextualized and illustrated formats. A light and easily understood sense of humor pervades all aspects of the presentation, making it thoroughly enjoyable and thereby indirectly reducing the stress of learning a new language.

The Characters of the Book

The characters who populate the pages of *Exploring English* are based on classic personality types. Through the use of such colorful characters, cultural types, ideals, and expectations are used to stimulate language use. For example, the characters are meant to represent appealing, universally recognized, and lovable types. The artist is typical of artists, relaxed in dress and yet passionate about his art. The banker is a staid and proper fellow, carrying all of the cultural expectations of a person to whom others entrust their life savings. The pilot is a woman of adventurous spirit, the doctor a caring woman of high principles. The absent-minded professor is an interesting man with esoteric interests and predictable habits. The children are typical of young people everywhere, interested in friends, sports, and having fun. The taxi driver and the mechanic, the restaurant owner and the waiter, the young married couple and the couple that have shared many years of married life, the secretary and the schoolteacher—all provide a wealth of language and human interest.

The interactions and the tensions between the characters also mirror real life. Their conversations provide ready models for students to understand and use in role play and real-life situations. The use of colorful characters and real personality types in common life situations enhances learning and enables the introduction of a broad range of functions and notions. Including real characters with a wide variety of personality types—some passionate about their work, some conservative, some just congenial people, others risk takers—enriches students' ability to talk about people both generally and specifically. The characters in *Exploring English* are not just bland generic "textbook" people whose names are inserted in sentences that teach vocabulary and grammar. Mr. Bascomb, Anne, Otis, and Dr. Pasto are people and types students have met and will continue to meet in their real lives.

HOW TO TEACH EACH PART OF A LESSON

The different parts of a lesson can be taught in a variety of ways. The suggestions that are given here are general and can be adapted to each Student Book page.

Conversations and Cartoon Stories

The Conversations can be introduced by having the students examine the pictures for clues first, then brainstorm words and ideas that they think will be needed, and then read or listen to the Conversation on the audiocassette tape. The class can be divided into groups to read the parts of individual characters along with the teacher or the tape, and individual students can play the parts using the very words of the text.

The Conversations and Cartoon Stories in *Exploring English* are dramatizations that can be used naturally as models for role playing. Students can adapt many of the dialogues to their own situations by substituting vocabulary items that they already know (or ask for help in learning). Be ready to help the students with words that they feel they need. Words learned in this way are almost always remembered the most easily because the need for the word is real to the students.

Pair Work

When students are directed to "Have similar conversations," they are being asked to role play. Only the students themselves know what language elements they have to use, so, by making up their own conversations, they are building on and building up their own reservoir of language. It is important to encourage students to share their role plays and also to provide the new words they want as they experiment with new words and grammar.

Students can greatly increase the amount of language they learn by working with a partner. You might decide to set up a rotation of partners so that students work with different partners each day or each week. You can accomplish this goal by making two teams of an approximately equal number of people. Make two disks of card stock, one a little larger than the other, large enough to write the names of the students of one team around the outside rim. Draw lines to divide the disk into equal pie sections. If one team has one more person, write that team's names on the larger disk. Write the names of the second team on the outside edge of the smaller disk. And match the partners for each day or each week by rotating the smaller disk by the amount of one person's name. If one team has an extra person, change who works in a triad each week.

Pair Work should always have a clear objective. One important objective and a goal of *Exploring English* is that students build on the Pair Work, using as much improvisation as possible with language they already know. It is always helpful for pairs who have been working together to show the rest of the class what language variations they have produced.

Structure and New Vocabulary

The direction "Listen and repeat" signals an opportunity to build students' aural skills. They need to learn to distinguish new sounds and words from similar ones they already know. They also need to listen to the teacher's model or the model on the tape to build the bridge between the spoken and the printed word.

The best way to introduce these exercises is to concentrate on the focus of the lesson by having the students listen to the model several times and then chant the model several times. In chorus or individually, the repetition makes familiar what was not familiar at all.

Practice

The oral Practice exercises provide a clear, close focus on the grammatical element that is being taught. Some of the oral Practice exercises require manipulation; the teacher presents the example or examples to the class and then asks the students to make the change requested in the exercise.

Some of these exercises require a transformation of part of the sentence, perhaps replacing proper names with appropriate personal pronouns.

Some of the exercises ask the students to manipulate sentences as a whole to practice different forms:

That is your pencil. → **That pencil is yours.**

Still other exercises are presented to help students learn to expand ideas:

Peter likes ketchup. (a bottle of ketchup) →
He wants a bottle of ketchup.

Another format for Practice asks the student to make an addition to the information in the first sentence. The student should read the first sentence and then make up a second sentence with the information that is provided:

Make sentences using **one** *and* **the other.**
I have two new shirts. (blue/green)
I have two new shirts. One is blue and the other is green.

Make negative sentences.
Tino and Barbara are eating sandwiches. (pizza)
They aren't eating pizza.

Make sentences using **have** + **any** *or* **one.**
Peter needs some gasoline.
He doesn't have any.

The Golos need a car.
They don't have one.

Exercises to stimulate question-asking may simply direct the students to do so:

Change the sentences to questions.
They're bankers.
Are they bankers?

Sometimes a substitution word may be given to use in forming the questions:

Make questions as indicated.
They don't have a desk. (a table)
Do they have a table?

*Make questions with **who**, **what**, or **where**.*
Albert went *to the beach.*
Where did he go?

Readings

Before you read the story or play the tape, spend a few moments with the students going over the illustration. What concepts do they expect to find in the reading as suggested in the picture or pictures? Brainstorming ideas will prepare the students for the activity; they will find it easier to process the content and concepts of the reading passage if they are mentally prepared by calling to consciousness the ideas they expect to find in the reading and being ready with at least some of the English labels for things. Remember, your students collectively may know a great deal of English language. The time you spend helping them to realize that they know words, that some words may be cognates or borrowings, and that there are relationships among the concepts will be well spent in making the lesson easier for them to comprehend. For example, on page 91, there is a drawing showing several recreational activities. If you ask the students what is in the picture and write the activities they see on the chalkboard, you won't have to do any more "teaching" of these words because they have already been provided by the students themselves.

Then read the story. You can read it yourself, play the tape, or do both. In any case, the students should hear the story several times, reading along silently or out loud as they follow the words in the textbook. If there are words or phrases that seem difficult for the students, stop and repeat the sentence several times. If necessary, use the backward build-up technique to keep the intonation and rhythm of the sentence true:

Wickam City is a wonderful place to live.
to live.
place to live.
a wonderful place to live.
Wickam City is a wonderful place to live.

Ask the students to write down the words that they don't know. Teach them the new items by acting them out or showing pictures. It is also acceptable to translate words occasionally or to consult a bilingual dictionary if other methods do not work efficiently.

Ask students different kinds of questions about the reading. Encourage them to use their own words in giving answers rather than searching in the text for the sentence that answers the question. As much as possible, include different kinds of questions: detail questions, main idea questions (for example, ask for key words or for a title for a reading), inferences (for example, how do you think [a character] feels about this situation? Or do you think [a character such as Mr. Bascomb] is a good banker?), definitions, and sequence questions. Also, ask your students personal questions that relate to the topic of the story in order to draw them into the story. If a story deals with shopping, ask your students about their own shopping, thus making the lesson a point of departure for class discussion.

It is important to stimulate real responses to the characters, to get the students to think about them as real personality types. The people in the textbook and the people in the class may be considered the English-speaking community for the learner. Through thoughtful questioning, you as the teacher can use the readings to simulate language use in society. When they laugh about Johnnie's indecisiveness on page 47, students are motivated to use language to explain what makes Tino's final observation funny.

What's Happening Here?

This section includes illustrated situations accompanied by audiotaped stories (on the reverse side of the page) that are designed to give the students practice in listening comprehension. As a rule, use the following procedure:

1. Have the students look at the illustration and describe what's happening in their own words. Prompt the students with questions if necessary.
2. Tell the students to continue looking at the illustration as they listen to the accompanying story. Then read the story or play the tape.
3. Ask the students to answer the comprehension questions that follow the story *while looking at the illustration*. Don't let the students turn the page and read the story. In order to get practice in listening comprehension, the students must respond to what they hear without referring to the text.

Grammar Summaries

At the end of Chapters 1, 2, 3, 5, 6, and 7 of the Student Book you will find Grammar Summaries. (Chapters 4 and 8 are review chapters.) These one-page presentations of the grammatical items in the chapter can be used in several ways.

The students can be referred to the Grammar Summaries throughout the lesson for an unencumbered presentation of the basic forms. Because of the differences in students' learning styles, you are likely to find that some students will frequently look to the Grammar Summary pages and others will hardly notice that they are there.

If your students are having difficulty with a grammatical structure, you can refer to the box on the Grammar Summary page that contains the problematic form. Show them how a slot-and-filler approach can work by writing the boxed sentences across the top of the board (not one under the other). Then—just like in the boxes on the Grammar Summary page—draw vertical lines between the sentence constituents; the subject should be separated from the verb phrase, the object noun phrase from the adverbials, etc. Show the students how to expand by adding or substituting other information: how a pronoun can substitute for the subject phrase, how elements within the verb phrase can change, and how different object nouns can be used in place of the original one. For some students, it might be useful to point out that one column is the subject, another the verb phrase, and so on. You can write under each heading all kinds of variations, brainstorming with the students or requiring a pair of students to come up with new sentences using this structure.

Suggestions for Teaching Pronunciation

The audiocassette tapes provide models for good pronunciation. If the students have trouble with certain sounds, play the tapes and have the students repeat the sentences after the voice on the tape. Pronunciation can be a lesson focus for five to ten minutes at any time that the students seem to need it. If the intonation patterns of your students' first languages interfere with natural-sounding English, you might want to introduce pronunciation at the beginning of the lesson. The tapes will be useful because natural intonation can be found there, and the same pattern can be repeated as many times as you need for your students to hear the music and cadence of English.

IMPORTANCE OF A PRELIMINARY ORAL PHASE: PRESENTATION AND WRITTEN REINFORCEMENT

Presentation

It's important that students hear examples of the sentences they are going to practice before they are asked to produce them. We refer to this step as the preliminary oral phase. The most effective preliminary oral phase requires care in the sequencing of the affirmative, interrogative, and negative forms of each structure presented. The following is a demonstration of the procedure, giving an abbreviated lesson teaching the simple past tense.

1. Introduce the structure with affirmative sentences. (A good way of teaching the simple past is by describing what you did this morning as you mime the various activities.)

   Teacher: This morning I got up at seven o'clock. I went to the bathroom and I took a shower. After I took a shower, I got dressed. Then I went to the kitchen and had breakfast. I had coffee and eggs for breakfast. After breakfast, I read the newspaper.

   Get students to make affirmative sentences by asking them information questions. (You can ask *or* questions, which are easier because they include the answer.)

   Teacher: _____, when did you get up this morning?
   Student: I got up at seven-thirty.

   Teacher: Did you take a bath or a shower?
   Student: I took a shower.

2. Give students practice in making information questions.

   Teacher: Listen. When did you get up this morning? Everyone!
   Students: When did you get up this morning?

   Have students ask each other information questions using *what, where, when, how,* etc.

   Teacher: (Student 1), ask (Student 2): When did you get up this morning?
   Student 1: (Student 2), when did you get up this morning?

3. Give examples of the negative form.

Teacher: I got up at seven o'clock. I didn't get up at six o'clock. I took a shower. I didn't take a bath. I had coffee and eggs for breakfast. I didn't have Coke and french fries. I didn't have pizza. I didn't have ice cream.

Ask students *Yes/No* questions that will elicit negative responses. (At this point, have students respond with complete sentences; the short answer comes later.)

Teacher: Listen. Did you have pizza for breakfast? Everyone!
Students: Did you have pizza for breakfast?

Have students ask each other *Yes/No* questions.

Teacher: (Student 1), ask (Student 2): Did you have pizza for breakfast?
Student 1: (Student 2), did you have pizza for breakfast?
Student 2: No, I didn't have pizza for breakfast.

4. Give examples of the short answer form.

Teacher: Did I have eggs for breakfast? Yes, I did. Did I have french fries for breakfast? No, I didn't.

Ask students questions that will elicit the short answer form.

Teacher: _____, did you take a shower this morning?
Student: Yes, I did.

Teacher: Did you watch TV this morning?
Student: No, I didn't.

Notice that all of the sentences in the demonstration above use *you* and *I*. When introducing new tenses, it's best to start with *you* and *I* before moving on to the third-person singular, since the third-person form requires an ending change that complicates initial presentation. Once students are comfortable with the structure, the third-person form can be introduced with success.

With other, simpler structures (*there is/there are, some/any,* etc.) the presentation can be shorter, but always maintain the sequencing of forms: affirmative, interrogative, negative, etc. It's always a good idea to limit the vocabulary in the preliminary oral work to familiar words and expressions and words whose meanings can be demonstrated through physical actions. Hand gestures are useful in telling students to listen, to repeat, to make complete sentences, etc.

Written Reinforcement

Your students can improve their understanding and retention of the structures they are practicing orally by writing them on the chalkboard—preferably after they have had a few minutes of preliminary oral work as in the demonstration above. For example, in the same lesson on the simple past tense, one student could ask another student, "What did you eat yesterday for breakfast?" The first student should then write the question on the chalkboard. After the second student answers, "I ate eggs," he or she should write this on the chalkboard. The students should continue writing their questions and answers until there are at least six to eight sentences in the simple past on the chalkboard. Number these sentences and have the class correct any mistakes in grammar and spelling. Avoid correcting the mistakes yourself; students learn more when they are actively involved in the correction process. At times you may need to guide your students, but usually they see the mistakes and are eager to correct them themselves. After all the corrections have been made, have the students read the sentences on the chalkboard, first in chorus and then individually.

DEVELOPING YOUR METHODOLOGY

To use this text effectively, the teacher is encouraged to use a variety of techniques. A productive pedagogical perspective is to recognize that acquisition and integration of new language is a process. This process has been engineered into the development of the text. What students can hear and understand, they can easily learn to say. What they can say and understand, they can also learn to read. What they can read, they can write. And then the circle begins again: What they can write, they can easily read and they can also learn to produce orally. For one student, the written word may seem easier to process for a while, and for another, the listening and speaking skills may advance more quickly; however, there will be a catch-up and evening-out of skills if all are taught in a manageable, integrated way. Thus, ultimately, the most effective approach is a general multiskill development focus.

Good teaching of the informed eclectic kind uses the best of many methods and the particular experience of the individual teacher. Some standard practices have become classics. The teacher models unfamiliar sounds and intonation patterns in sentences; the students listen and then imitate the teacher. The teacher shows how to do something and then the students try it out in role play. New elements are presented through as many channels as possible:

The visual channel is used in the pictures and the print in the book, in written words and sentences on the chalkboard.

The auditory channel is used as the students listen to the teacher reading, to the tape presentations, and to their fellow students.

The kinesthetic channel is used as the students manipulate items of realia, write on the chalkboard or in their journals, and participate in games and role plays.

CORRECTING ERRORS

Errors can be considered "mis-takes." The student might well know how to say something correctly, but his or her competence in the language may not always match the performance. Therefore, be judicious and gentle in correcting students' language. You might want to draw their attention to the most important problems, those that interfere with communication. For example, if a student's mispronunciation of the short vowel in *ship* makes the word sound like *sheep* and the context is clearly nautical, there will probably not be any difficulty with understanding the message. However, if the context is not clear, then the teacher may ask the student to listen to a model of the two words, listen to be able to hear the difference, and then have the student attempt a more accurate pronunciation.

In oral work, make corrections by giving a student a chance to redo his or her own work. For example, you might ask the student, "Is that the right way to make a question with a *Yes/No* answer?" Or, if you think the student is still learning how to form the desired utterance, and the student makes a small mistake, you can just work a correct repetition of the form or structure into your next utterance. Look at this example:

Student: Who that is?
Teacher: Who is that? I don't know. Let's ask . . .

Note that it is generally not a good idea to ask one student to correct another. If a student doesn't know the answer to a question, the student might well be embarrassed. You can provide students with coping strategies in an early lesson: "I don't know. Why don't you ask . . . ?" A student who learns early to ask another student for an answer always feels in control of his or her language-learning situation. Such a student is less likely to feel frustrated and anxious.

HOW TO PLAN A COURSE SYLLABUS

It is important for a teacher to know how much time to spend on each part of a lesson and how to fit the text materials into a time frame. If your class meets for an hour a day, five days a week, through a sixteen-week semester, it is easy to gauge the amount of time: eight lessons in sixteen weeks means one chapter every two weeks. If your class meets frequently for longer periods of time, you must adjust the material and the time to each other; you might be able to complete a chapter in a week, for example, if you meet for two to three hours a day every day.

The more your students practice with vocabulary and grammatical elements, the more natural their use of the language elements will be. For the reinforcement of some elements, you may find it useful to return to a completed chapter and have the students read passages aloud, answer questions, expand on the topic, or combine elements. A useful exercise for students who are quick to learn is to have them revise (rewrite) the stories of earlier chapters, incorporating elements from later chapters into more sophisticated sentences.

By recognizing that a textbook like *Exploring English* can be expanded and that the material is flexible, you can make the text fit your teaching situation and your schedule.

SUGGESTIONS FOR SETTING UP THE CLASSROOM

The object of a good language lesson is to keep the students engaged and involved. Some general suggestions, included here, will help you to make your classroom a dynamic and energy-filled learning environment.

The Arrangement of Desks

Ideal for a language classroom is an arrangement of desks that makes pair work and group work natural. Movable tables and chairs work well if they are arranged in a horseshoe or circular pattern or in slanted rows like a *V* with the point of the *V* farthest from the teacher and the chalkboard. Another possible arrangement is to make clusters of desks: Individual student desks can be arranged in sets of four, facing one another but allowing for a clear view of the chalkboard in the front of the room.

Classroom Paraphernalia and Decorations

There are many ways to enrich the experience of *Exploring English*. For example, besides chalkboards or dry-erase whiteboards, ideal classrooms contain bulletin boards for posting student work and realia of relevant types (pictures, forms, labels, etc.); wall space for charts and maps; a large calendar; shelves for books and magazines; boxes to store supplies of paper, pencils, colored markers, tape, and scissors; and boxes for manipulable learning aids such as picture files, English-language greeting cards and travel brochures, color samples, examples of texture, colored chalk, plastic fruit and vegetables, Cuisenaire rods and blocks, play money, sample forms of all kinds like checks and receipts, and a mock clock to teach telling time. The idea is to use these items in ways that help create a rich English-language environment within the classroom.

If a teacher works with students to keep developing the displays of English language in use (through, for example, a bulletin board display for a holiday done in English and including symbols of the holiday and greeting cards), the students will have access to more than just the language—they will begin to participate in the culture of their new language.

Chalkboard (or Whiteboard) Use

Even before your students open the textbook, you might want to have them become comfortable writing on the chalkboard. You can begin by writing your name and then having the students write theirs. Familiarity and comfort with writing on the chalkboard do not always come easily to students, and shy students need to be introduced to the concept in an anxiety-free way. As you get them to write more and more on the chalkboard, they will find that it offers advantages: One has more time to think, and other students help with the idea to be expressed.

Summary of Contents

Chapter 1   1

TOPICS
Politics
Meeting people
Movies

GRAMMAR
Present perfect continuous
Verb + gerund
Gerund as subject

FUNCTIONS
Talking about things people have been doing
Expressing likes and dislikes
Giving opinions
Telling a story
Predicting

Chapter 2   5

TOPICS
Leisure activities
Gripes
Weddings
Children
Marriage

GRAMMAR
First conditional
Defining relative clauses with "whose"
    and "where"
Noun clauses

FUNCTIONS
Expressing probability
Asking for and giving information
Expressing dissatisfaction
Persuading

Chapter 3   10

TOPICS
Health care
Money
Sports
Friendship

GRAMMAR
Was able to/will be able to
May/might
Verbs of perception

FUNCTIONS
Talking about ability in the past and future
Expressing possibility
Describing people and things
Talking about future plans
Expressing opinions

Chapter 4   16

TOPICS
Dating
Finding a job
Meeting people
Politics

GRAMMAR
Review

FUNCTIONS
Making comparisons
Starting a conversation
Inviting someone out
Giving opinions
Making suggestions
Expressing intention

Chapter 5   22

TOPICS
Military service
Jobs
Leisure activities
Exercise

GRAMMAR
Had to/will have to
Verb + object + infinitive (with "to")
Would rather

FUNCTIONS
Talking about obligation in the past
   and future
Interviewing for a job
Expressing preference
Making conclusions
Giving opinions

Chapter 6   27

TOPICS
Places to live
Juvenile delinquency
Work

GRAMMAR
Second conditional
So + adjective/such + noun
Reflexive pronouns

FUNCTIONS
Expressing possibility and probability
Making wishes
Talking about consequences
Giving advice
Persuading

Chapter 7   33

TOPICS
Housing
The legal system
Dreams

GRAMMAR
Gerunds

FUNCTIONS
Criticizing
Asking for and giving directions
Telling a story
Describing people
Talking about dreams
Renting an apartment

Chapter 8   38

TOPICS
Leisure activities
Proverbs
Current issues
Problems at work

GRAMMAR
Review

FUNCTIONS
Describing experiences
Making comparisons
Agreeing and disagreeing
Giving reasons
Solving problems
Talking about feelings/emotions
Recommending
Giving opinions

►PRELIMINARY ORAL WORK

Present Perfect Continuous (pp. 3–6)

We use this tense for an action that began in the past and is still continuing, or has only just finished:

> I've been watching TV.
> She's been painting the kitchen.

The present perfect continuous is formed by the present perfect of *to be* + present participle:

> He's been working hard.
> They've been saving their money.

It is often used with time expressions such as *recently, this afternoon, all day,* etc., when these expressions mean a period of time that is not finished or has only just finished:

> She's been calling me all week.
> We've been going out a lot recently.

The simple present perfect can also express an action that began in the past and leads up to the present. When used in this way it is very much like the present perfect continuous, and either form can be used:

> You've worked at the bank for a long time.
> You've been working at the bank for a long time.

Note: With verbs that are not used in the continuous forms, the present perfect continuous could not replace the simple present perfect:

> She's been at the library since ten o'clock.
> I've known her all my life.

Ask students questions using the present perfect continuous:

Teacher:	I've been living in this city for six years. How long have you been living here?
Student:	I've been living here for one year.

How long have you been studying English?
How long have you been coming to this school?
How long have you been using this book?
How long have you been sitting in that chair?

Get students to ask each other questions using the present perfect continuous:

Teacher:	Ask your partner how long he or she has been studying English.
Student A:	How long have you been studying English?
Student B:	I've been studying English for two years.

Verb + Gerund (pp. 7–10)

The gerund must be used after certain verbs:

> I keep forgetting your sister's name.
> We finished cleaning the house.

See page 162 in the appendix for a list of verbs that take the gerund.

Ask students questions using verb + gerund:

Teacher:	I enjoy playing tennis. What do you enjoy doing?
Student:	I enjoy listening to music.

Introduce other verbs that are followed by the gerund:

like	finish	stop
dislike	keep	love
avoid	start	hate

CHAPTER I

► ANSWERS

Reading 1 (p. 4)

1. Mr. Bascomb has been running for office since last year.
2. He wants to bring more business to the city and has promised to build a toy factory in City Park.
3. Yes, he has been spending a lot of money to win the election.
4. So far, he has spent over $50,000.

Reading 2 (p. 4)

1. Otis has been campaigning for a few months.
2. He is more concerned about the environment than the economy.
3. He has promised to save City Park.
4. Otis has very little money to spend on his campaign, but he has a lot of volunteers.

Written Exercise (p. 4)

1. Albert <u>has been studying</u> at the university for two years now.
2. He <u>has been driving</u> a car since he was sixteen.
3. We <u>have been having</u> some beautiful weather this month.
4. Linda <u>has been spending</u> a lot of time at the beach.
5. I <u>have been writing</u> some letters to my family.
6. You <u>have been watching</u> too much television.
7. Our basketball team <u>has been winning</u> a lot of games.
8. The boys <u>have been playing</u> hard this year.

Practice 1 (p. 6)

1. I've been making a lot of speeches.
2. I've been holding a lot of meetings.
3. I've been giving a lot of interviews.
4. I've been talking to a lot of voters.
5. I've been shaking a lot of hands.
6. I've been kissing a lot of babies.
7. I've been making a lot of promises.
8. I've been hiring a lot of campaign workers.
9. I've been buying a lot of advertisements.

Practice 2 (p. 6)

Answers will vary.

Practice 3 (p. 6)

Answers will vary.

Practice 4 (p. 6)

Answers will vary.

Reading 1 (p. 8)

1. Anne has been working at City Bank for two years.
2. She doesn't like working for him because she thinks he's a difficult man. She hates typing and she can't stand taking orders.

3. She hates typing because it's so boring.
4. She says, "I can't go on doing this work. It's driving me crazy."
5. Music is the most important thing in her life.
6. She loves singing and playing the guitar.

Reading 2 (p. 8)

1. Barbara has been working at the bank a little longer than Anne.
2. No, they don't have the same attitude about their jobs.
3. Barbara really enjoys working at the bank.
4. If Barbara wanted to, she could work with her husband, Tino, at the Martinoli Restaurant.
5. She prefers working at the bank because she likes it, she's learning a lot, and she has a good future.

Practice (p. 8)

1. I don't mind spending money.
   or I avoid spending money.
   or I can't stand spending money.
2. I don't mind listening to music.
   or I avoid listening to music.
   or I can't stand listening to music.
3. I don't mind doing homework.
   or I avoid doing homework.
   or I can't stand doing homework.
4. I don't mind studying at night.
   or I avoid studying at night.
   or I can't stand studying at night.
5. I don't mind getting up early.
   or I avoid getting up early.
   or I can't stand getting up early.
6. I don't mind taking the bus.
   or I avoid taking the bus.
   or I can't stand taking the bus.
7. I don't mind going to the market.
   or I avoid going to the market.
   or I can't stand going to the market.
8. I don't mind making dinner.
   or I avoid making dinner.
   or I can't stand making dinner.
9. I don't mind eating fried food.
   or I avoid eating fried food.
   or I can't stand eating fried food.
10. I don't mind washing the dishes.
    or I avoid washing the dishes.
    or I can't stand washing the dishes.

Pair Work (p. 10)

Answers will vary.

Story Questions (p. 13)

Answers may vary.

1. He met her when he was driving his taxi.
2. He was happy to meet her because he was a real fan of hers.

3. Ula Hackey thought that he was very pleasant.
4. He was different from most people because it didn't seem to bother him at all to talk to Ula.
5. Barney's favorite story was about a man who didn't have any money and tried to pay his fare with cigars.
6. The police officer stopped Barney because Barney went right through a stop light.
7. Answers will vary. I think Barney didn't see the stop light because he was talking too much.
8. The police officer gave Barney a ticket.
9. First Miss Hackey offered to do the talking, then she offered to pay the ticket for Barney.
10. Barney didn't accept because he was doing the driving.
11. Miss Hackey offered him the part of a taxi driver in her new movie.
12. Barney felt better and he accepted the offer.
13. Answers will vary.

Practice 1 (p. 13)
1. Eating out is expensive.
2. Saving money is difficult.
3. Taking the bus is economical.
4. Helping others is important.
5. Making new friends is wonderful.
6. Being in love is fantastic.
7. Being a good loser is difficult.
8. Riding a bicycle is easy.
9. Dancing is fun.

Practice 2 (p. 13)
Answers will vary.

Written Exercise (p. 14)
Answers will vary.

Pair Work (p. 14)
1. A: I'd like a cup of coffee.
   B: So would I.
2. A: I don't watch TV very much.
   B: Neither do I.
3. A: I went shopping yesterday.
   B: So did I.
4. A: I'm tired.
   B: So am I.
5. A: I couldn't sleep last night.
   B: Neither could I.
6. A: I won't be here Saturday.
   B: Neither will I.
7. A: I have a lot of things to do.
   B: So do I.
8. A: I've always been very busy.
   B: So have I.
9. A: I'm never bored.
   B: Neither am I.

Pair Work (p. 15)
1. A: What has Suzi been doing?
   B: She's been picking flowers.
2. A: What have Otis and Gloria been doing?
   B: They've been riding bicycles.
3. A: What have Barbara and Tino been doing?
   B: They've been playing tennis.
4. A: What has Nick been doing?
   B: He's been working on his car.
5. A: What have Peter and Maria been doing?
   B: They've been swimming.
6. A: What has Linda been doing?
   B: She's been studying.
7. A: What has Fred been doing?
   B: He's been sleeping.
8. A: What have Cathy and Danny been doing?
   B: They've been kissing.

"Movies" Questions (p. 17)
Answers may vary.

1. People go to the movies to escape their normal everyday existence and to experience a life more exciting than their own.
2. American movies are popular because they tell interesting stories and are well made.
3. Charlie Chaplin, Humphrey Bogart, Marilyn Monroe, Arnold Schwarzenegger, and Tom Hanks are some famous Hollywood stars.
4. We need movie heroes because they do things the average person would like to do but often can't.
5. Making movies is a very risky business, since seven times out of ten, producers are unsuccessful and their movies lose money.
6. Hollywood produces many different kinds of films, including mysteries, comedies, musicals, love stories, and horror films.
7. Conflict is the heart of drama.
8. Opposition creates conflict. (Answers may vary.) For example, a protagonist is a young man from the wrong side of the tracks who wants to marry the beautiful daughter of a rich banker. The father thinks the young man is unworthy of his daughter, and he forbids her to see him.
9. In a good movie, the main character learns something from his experiences that makes him a different, perhaps better, person.
10. Movies help us understand a little more about life.

Free Response (p. 17)
Answers will vary.

Group Work and Class Activity (p. 18)
Answers will vary.

Talking about Politics, Group Work, and Talking about Meeting People (p. 19)
Answers will vary.

WORKBOOK EXERCISES

▶ANSWERS

Exercise 1 (pp. 1–2)
1. She's been picking flowers.
2. They've been swimming.
3. They've been eating.
4. She's been watching television.
5. She's been crying.
6. They've been fighting.
7. He's been painting the house.
8. He's been repairing the car.
9. She's been shopping.
10. They've been playing football.
11. She's been ironing clothes.
12. He's been cutting the grass.
13. They've been washing the car.
14. He's been sleeping.
15. She's been flying an airplane.
16. They've been kissing.

Exercise 2 (p. 3)
1. So could you.
2. So are we.
3. Neither does he.
4. Neither can they.
5. So would everyone else.
6. Neither is your sister.
7. So will I.
8. Neither have we.
9. Neither did she.
10. So was I.
11. So has he.
12. So do you.
13. Neither is she.
14. Neither do we.
15. So can I.

Exercise 3 (p. 3)
Answers will vary.

Exercise 4 (p. 4)
Answers will vary.

Exercise 5 (p. 4)
Answers will vary.

Exercise 6 (p. 5)
1. Anne is doing the typing.
2. Sam is doing the gardening.
3. Dr. Pasto is doing the cooking.
4. Jimmy is doing the ironing.
5. Mrs. Golo is doing the shopping.
6. Gloria is doing the painting.
7. Mrs. Hamby is doing the talking.

Exercise 7 (p. 6)
1. He started going out with her a few months ago.
2. He stopped calling us a few months ago.
3. She started washing her hair with eggs a few months ago.
4. She stopped using shampoo a few months ago.
5. He started growing a beard a few months ago.
6. He stopped shaving a few months ago.
7. She started driving a few months ago.
8. She stopped taking the bus a few months ago.
9. I started eating at the Martinoli Restaurant a few months ago.
10. I stopped eating at Joe's Cafe a few months ago.

Exercise 8 (p. 7)
1. I have known them for years.
2. They have lived in Atlanta all their lives.
3. Laura bought a cookbook a few days ago.
4. The first thing she made was an apple pie.
5. We had dinner at the Carsons' last night.
6. We have been to their house three times this week.
7. She has gone out for the day.
8. She left about fifteen minutes ago.
9. Frank repaired the roof yesterday.
10. He has made a lot of improvements in the house lately.

Exercise 9 (p. 7)
Answers may vary.

1. I'm not lucky enough.
2. Gloria tried to lift that heavy box, but she wasn't strong enough.
3. You're a good singer, but you don't sing well enough to be a professional.
4. They weren't speaking loudly enough.
5. It isn't big enough.
6. She isn't tall enough.
7. He doesn't study hard enough.
8. She didn't run fast enough.
9. He isn't old enough.
10. You don't write clearly enough.

Exercise 10 (p. 8)
Composition

▶**PRELIMINARY ORAL WORK**

First Conditional (pp. 23–26)

The verb in the *if*-clause is in the present tense; the verb in the main clause is in the future:

> If she goes to the party, she'll have a good time.
> If you give me your telephone number, I'll call you tomorrow.

If the action in the *if*-clause is performed, it is quite probable that the action in the main clause will be performed.

> *Unless* + affirmative verb = *if* + negative verb:

> We'll go to the park unless it rains (if it doesn't rain).
> Unless you leave now (if you don't leave now), you'll miss the bus.

Ask students questions using the first conditional:

Teacher:	What'll you do if it rains this weekend?
Student:	I'll stay home.
Teacher:	What'll you do if the weather is good?
Student:	I'll go to the beach.

Have students complete sentences of the type given below:

> If Fred finds a job, he'll be very happy.

> If Peter drives too fast, . . .
> If your friends come to the party, . . .
> If you eat too much, . . .
> If you're nice to Mr. Bascomb, . . .
> If you ask him for money, . . .
> If Jane works hard, . . .
> If you ask her for her phone number, . . .
> If Mr. Dole comes late to work one more time, . . .
> If Linda studies, . . .
> If you stay in the sun too long, . . .
> If you take my advice, . . .
> If you help me, . . .

Relative Clauses with "Whose" and "Where" (pp. 27–30)

We use *whose* to show possession:

> That's the boy whose mother is a professional dancer.
> I saw a cat whose eyes were green and blue.

We use *where* when talking about a place:

> That's the restaurant where I met Jane.
> The street where she lives is very quiet.

Have students combine sentences using *whose:*

Teacher:	We know a man. His car is pink. We know a man whose car is pink.
	We know a girl. Her father is an actor.
Student:	We know a girl whose father is an actor.

Have students combine sentences using *where:*

Teacher:	That's the street. They had the accident there. That's the street where they had the accident.
	That's the park. We play football there.
Student:	That's the park where we play football.

Noun Clauses

In each of the following sentences the object is a noun clause:

> Do you remember what he said?
> She knows how to write a business letter.
> I don't understand why they sold their car.

What, who, where, when, why, and *how* are used to introduce noun clauses.

Have students complete sentences of the type given below using noun clauses:

> I don't know where the dictionary is.

> I wonder . . .
> I don't remember . . .
> I know . . .
> I don't understand . . .

Noun clauses with the verb *to be:*

> That's why I didn't come to the meeting.
> That was how she met him.
> City Park is where they're having the picnic.

Have students make sentences using noun clauses with the verb *to be.*

CHAPTER 2

► ANSWERS

Reading 1 (p. 24)
1. Tino and his friends are at the sporting goods store.
2. They are planning a fishing trip to Bear Lake.
3. There has been a lot of rain recently.
4. Barbara wants to paint the living room this weekend.
5. Yes, he promised to help her.
6. If it rains, Tino will stay home and help his wife.
7. If the weather is good, he'll go fishing.

Reading 2 (p. 24)
1. Peter loves to visit foreign countries and go out with beautiful women.
2. No, he has never gotten married.
3. He enjoys his freedom as a bachelor.
4. If he gets married some day, he will have to stop traveling so much.
5. If he remains a bachelor, he will keep on traveling and going out with beautiful women.

Practice (p. 24)
1. Anne would like to learn Spanish. If she goes to Mexico, she'll learn Spanish.
2. Mr. Bascomb hopes to build a factory in City Park. If he becomes mayor, he'll build a factory in City Park.
3. Otis promised to save the park. If he becomes mayor, he'll save the park.
4. Jimmy and Linda want to go to the beach. If it's a nice day, they'll go to the beach.
5. Jack wants to buy a new car. If he gets the money, he'll buy a new car.
6. Mrs. Brown promised to get some tomatoes. If she goes to the market, she'll get some tomatoes.
7. I would like to visit the Art Museum. If I have time, I'll visit the Art Museum.
8. My friends would like to watch television. If they go home, they'll watch television.
9. Fred is trying to find a job. If he keeps trying, he'll find a job.

Pair Work (p. 26)
Answers will vary.

Practice (p. 28)
1. I talked to a boy whose father is a salesman.
2. He works for a woman whose only interest is making money.
3. We know a girl whose brother lives in France.
4. They have a friend whose family is very rich.
5. We heard about a man whose favorite pastime is eating.
6. He married a woman whose favorite pastime is cooking.
7. I'm thinking of a girl whose eyes are different colors.
8. She's going out with a boy whose family comes from New York.

Pair Work (p. 28)
Answers will vary.

Written Exercise (p. 30)
1. How much does this book cost? Can you tell me _how much this book costs_ ?
2. What did you say? I didn't hear _what you said_ .
3. Are they coming to the party? I wonder _if they're coming to the party_
4. Do we have their phone number? I'm not sure _if we have their phone number_
5. How does this machine work? Could you explain _how this machine works_ ?
6. Where did I leave the key? I can't remember _where I left the key_ .
7. Why are you so upset? I don't understand _why you're so upset_ .
8. Is something wrong? Please tell me _if something's wrong_ .
9. Did anyone call the police? Do you know _if anyone called the police_ ?

Pair Work (p. 30)
"B" answers will vary.

1. A: Do you know where the nearest library is?
   B: Yes. It's on Bond Street.
      or I'm not sure. I think there's one on Franklin Avenue.
      or Sorry. I have no idea.
2. A: Do you know if the library is open on Saturday.
3. A: Do you know if the teacher has a dictionary?
4. A: Do you know what the word "bachelor" means?
5. A: Do you know where I can get some envelopes?
6. A: Do you know when the post office closes?
7. A: Do you know how much an airmail stamp costs?

Story Questions (p. 33)
1. Mr. Bascomb made an important speech.
2. He called himself a native son because he was born and grew up in Wickam City.
3. According to Mr. Bascomb, the main issues in the campaign are jobs and taxes.

4. According to Mr. Bascomb, the economy of Wickam City is in bad shape and it's getting worse.
5. He wants to build a toy factory in City Park because it will provide more jobs and tax money.
6. Mr. Jackson says they should not build a factory in City Park. He wants to keep the park as it is.
7. If the toy company owners don't get permission to use City Park, they'll build their factory in another city.
8. If there is no new business in Wickam City, they will have more unemployment and higher taxes.
9. Answers will vary.
10. Answers will vary.

Practice (p. 33)
1. He was on TV yesterday, wasn't he?
2. You didn't see him, did you?
3. You haven't talked to him, have you?
4. He's a very busy man, isn't he?
5. He doesn't have much free time, does he?
6. He wants to build a factory in City Park, doesn't he?
7. The park isn't a good place for a factory, is it?
8. Most people disagree with Mr. Bascomb, don't they?
9. He won't succeed, will he?

Written Exercise (p. 33)
Answers will vary.

Written Exercise 1 (p. 34)
1. We have a friend __whose__ parents live in a beautiful house by the beach.
2. You can understand __why__ they spend a lot of time there.
3. Fred is worried because he doesn't know __what__ to do with his life.
4. He'll certainly feel better __when__ he finds a job.
5. The girl __whose__ team lost the basketball game was very unhappy.
6. She left in a hurry and didn't tell anyone __where__ she went.
7. I had my keys __when__ I left the house this morning, but now I can't find them.
8. I wonder __where__ I put my keys.

Written Exercise 2 (p. 34)
1. That's the market where we used to shop.
2. The dinner that your mother made was delicious.

3. Do you know who this radio belongs to?
4. I met the woman whose son you were talking about.
5. I'd like to find out where they live.
6. Could you tell me what time it is?
7. Let's find a place where we can have a quiet conversation.
8. Do you know if there is a coffee shop nearby?

Group Work 1 (p. 35)
Answers will vary.

Group Work 2 (p. 35)
Answers will vary.

"American Weddings" Questions (p. 37)
Answers may vary.

1. The many different kinds of weddings reflect the different religious and ethnic backgrounds of the American people.
2. An overwhelming majority of today's couples choose to marry in a traditional religious ceremony.
3. When the bride enters the church or synagogue, everyone stands up.
4. The groom and the officiant wait for the bride at the end of the aisle.
5. After they exchange rings, they kiss.
6. After the ceremony, everyone goes outside, and the guests rush up to congratulate the couple and wish them well.
7. The reception is an opportunity for family and friends to share the joy of the bride and groom. There is food, drink, and music to make everyone relaxed and happy.
8. The first dance is reserved for the bride and groom. After that, the rest of the bridal party joins in and the guests may follow.
9. The bride and groom together make the first cut in the wedding cake.
10. Supposedly, the one who catches it will be the next to get married.
11. After the wedding, the couple drives off in the groom's car.

Free Response (p. 37)
Answers will vary.

Talking about Children, Group Work, and Talking about Marriage (p. 38)
Answers will vary.

WORKBOOK EXERCISES

▶**ANSWERS**

Exercise 1 (p. 11)
1. If she practices every day, she'll be a good tennis player.
2. If he starts exercising, he'll lose weight.
3. If she takes care of herself, she'll live a long life.
4. If he helps others, he'll be popular.
5. If she talks to Mr. Bascomb, she'll get a raise in pay.
6. If he studies, he'll pass the test.
7. If she leaves now, she'll catch the eight o'clock bus.
8. If he goes to the employment agency, he'll get a job.
9. If he wears a coat and tie, he'll make a good impression.
10. If she goes to the beach every day, she'll get a suntan.

Exercise 2 (p. 12)
Answers will vary.

Exercise 3 (p. 12)
Answers will vary.

Exercise 4 (p. 12)
Answers will vary.

Exercise 5 (p. 13)
"Howdy, stranger. Sit down and have a cup of coffee. There's something I want to tell you. I have a friend <u>whose</u> horse was stolen yesterday. He left his horse <u>by the river</u> <u>where</u> the old miner used to live. Some people think <u>he's</u> the one <u>who</u> stole the horse. But nobody was there <u>when</u> it happened, so they can't say for sure <u>who</u> did it. As for me, I really don't know <u>what</u> to think. I don't understand <u>why</u> anyone would take something that didn't belong to them. But I'll tell you one thing. The person <u>who</u> stole the horse will be very sorry <u>when</u> my friend catches him. My friend is the local sheriff, and he has a mean, vicious dog <u>whose</u> favorite pastime is tracking down criminals. This is a town <u>where</u> horse thieves receive the worst kind of <u>punishment</u>, you know. That's <u>why</u> someone made a big mistake <u>when</u> they stole the sheriff's horse. I hope you've <u>been</u> listening to <u>what</u> I've been saying, stranger. Nobody around here knows <u>who</u> you are, and they might even suspect you of being the thief. That's <u>why</u> you should get out of town on the next train. You don't want to be a man <u>whose</u> first visit to this town was his last, do you? Hope you don't mind a little friendly advice. So long, stranger."

Exercise 6 (p. 14)
1. She <u>gets along with</u> everyone.
2. She still knows <u>quite a few</u> people there.
3. If you don't leave <u>right away</u>, you're going to be late.
4. Let's <u>talk it over</u> after work.
5. We <u>think a lot of</u> her.
6. She has been expecting some letters, but <u>so far</u> she hasn't received any.
7. You really have to <u>pay attention</u> to understand him.
8. <u>No wonder</u> he looks tired.
9. <u>He's in a bad mood</u>.
10. You should <u>take it easy</u>.
11. You can always <u>count on</u> me.
12. <u>From now on</u> I'm taking the bus.

Exercise 7 (p. 14)
Answers will vary.

Exercise 8 (p. 15)
1. Linda is a student <u>at</u> Wickam University.
2. She usually studies <u>in</u> her room.
3. There's a good movie <u>at</u> the Odeon this week.
4. The Odeon is <u>on</u> Central Avenue.
5. Anne lives <u>in</u> a small house <u>at</u> the end of the street.
6. Would you like to live <u>on</u> a farm <u>in</u> the country?
7. We're going to spend our next vacation <u>on</u> an island <u>in</u> the South Pacific.
8. Mr. Dole isn't feeling well today. He's <u>at</u> home <u>in</u> bed.
9. His office is <u>on</u> the second floor of the Barnett Building.

Exercise 9 (p. 15)
1. There weren't <u>many</u> people at the party last night.
2. It was a boring party. There <u>wasn't</u> much food or entertainment.
3. It cost <u>a lot of</u> money to have a big party.
4. You look <u>a little</u> tired. How <u>much</u> sleep did you get last night?
5. Peter is taking a coffee break. He'll be back in <u>a few</u> minutes.
6. He drinks <u>a lot of</u> coffee, at least five cups a day.
7. He only puts <u>a little</u> sugar in his coffee. He doesn't like it <u>too</u> sweet.
8. Mr. Dupont doesn't speak <u>much</u> English, only <u>a few</u> words.
9. I can speak <u>a little</u> French, enough to carry on a short conversation.
10. How <u>many</u> languages can you speak?

Exercise 10 (p. 16)
1. A blonde woman <u>just</u> came out of the bank.
2. She ran <u>quickly</u> across the street.
3. Then a police officer stopped her.

4. He <u>probably</u> thought she was a bank robber.
5. <u>Unfortunately</u>, she had no identification.
6. She smiled <u>sweetly</u> at the police officer.
7. He thought she was <u>very</u> beautiful.
8. He <u>really</u> wanted to talk with her.
9. <u>Suddenly</u>, a limousine pulled up at the curb.
   or A limousine <u>suddenly</u> pulled up at the curb.
10. "I have to go <u>now</u>," said the woman.

11. "Maybe we'll meet <u>again</u> someday."
12. "I <u>sure</u> hope so," said the police officer.

Exercise 11 (p. 16)
Answers will vary.

Exercise 12 (pp. 17–18)
Composition

► **PRELIMINARY ORAL WORK**

Will Be Able to/Was Able to (pp. 42–46)

To be able to is similar in meaning to *can* and provides an alternative form for the present and past tenses:

> She can work. = She is able to work.
> She could work. = She was able to work.

Could and *was able* are used for past ability:

> He could/was able to dance all night.

For ability and a particular action, use *was able to*:

> Although I had a headache, I was able to finish my homework.
> Although the suitcase was heavy, he was able to carry it.

Can indicates future time when it is used with time expressions such as *tomorrow, next week,* etc.:

> We can go to the beach tomorrow.

In cases where ability will exist only eventually, or where it is dependent on some other event in the future, we use *will be able to*:

> We'll be able to go to the beach when the weather gets warmer.

Have students complete sentences of the type given below using *was able to*:

> Although the coffee was hot, I was able to drink it.

> Although the suitcase was heavy, . . .
> Although the dress was expensive, . . .
> Although the car was in bad condition, . . .
> Although her address wasn't in the telephone book, . . .
> Although the food wasn't very good, . . .
> Although the door was locked, . . .
> Although his English wasn't very good, . . .
> Although the shirt was a little big for me, . . .
> Although she was asking a lot of money for her house, . . .
> Although he didn't have much time, . . .
> Although she didn't have a map, . . .

May/Might (pp. 47–50)

We use *may* in questions to ask for permission:

> May I use your pen?

When used in statements *may* indicates possibility:

> Our team may win the football game.
> I may go out tonight.

Have students make sentences using *may*:

> It's possible he'll buy a new TV.
> He may buy a new TV.

> It's possible they'll sell their car.
> It's possible she'll go to the party.
> It's possible we'll have rain tomorrow.
> It's possible he'll walk to work.
> It's possible they'll have lunch at Joe's Cafe.
> It's possible they'll have lunch at home.
> It's possible our team will win the football game.
> It's possible we'll take our vacation next month.
> It's possible we'll go to Hawaii.
> It's possible we'll stay at the Hilton Hotel.

Might, like *may,* usually indicates a possible action in the future. Their meaning is very similar, but we are less sure with *might*:

> It might rain tomorrow.
> They might buy a new car.

Have students make sentences using *might*:

> Don't leave your money on the table.
> Someone might take it.

> Don't criticize Barbara.
> Don't loan your camera to Fred.
> Don't sell your car.
> Don't eat too much cake.
> Don't stand on the table.
> Don't drive too fast.
> Don't park your car on the sidewalk.
> Don't leave your keys in the car.
> Don't forget to carry a map when you visit a strange city.

Verbs of Perception

Some of the most common linking verbs are *look, sound, feel, taste,* and *smell*. These verbs are usually followed by adjectives:

> This coffee tastes good.
> Your sweater feels soft.

Linking verbs can be followed by nouns if *like* is placed between the verb and the noun:

> He looks like a cowboy.
> She sounds like a professional singer.

Write these verbs on the chalkboard: *look, smell, sound, feel,* and *taste*.

Have students complete the following sentences using linking verb + adjective:

This soup tastes good.

This perfume . . .
Your stereo . . .
That photo . . .
This bed . . .
Your apartment . . .
Those flowers . . .
A hot shower . . .

These cookies . . .
That music . . .
Your suitcase . . .

As If/As Though/Like

As if, as though, and *like* have the same meaning. They each introduce a clause that may or may not be true:

He talks as if he has a lot of money.
She looks as though she were an actress.
I feel like I'm getting a cold.

CHAPTER 3

▶ ANSWERS

Reading (p. 44)

1. Nancy was flying with a sign saying OTIS FOR MAYOR.
2. As she was going back to the airport, her right engine began to sputter. It died in less than a minute.
3. Yes, she became frightened when the plane started losing altitude.
4. She tried to land in a wheat field.
5. She wasn't able to land where she wanted to because her plane was going too fast.
6. She crashed into a barn.
7. The barn belonged to Elmer Coggins.
8. He was feeding his chickens when he heard the crash.
9. He found Nancy inside the plane.
10. She had a concussion and a broken leg.
11. Elmer opened the door of the plane and gently pulled her out. He laid Nancy on a pile of hay and tried to make her comfortable. Then he ran to the farmhouse and called an ambulance.

Written Exercise (p. 44)

1. Although he was poor, he __was able to__ go to college.
2. He didn't know anyone at the bank, but he __was able to__ get a loan.
3. We were so busy last week we __weren't able to__ come to your party.
4. Although I had a headache, I __was able to__ do my homework.
5. She had no money, so she __wasn't able to__ buy a present for her mother.
6. Her apartment was so small she __wasn't able to__ invite her friends over for dinner.
7. Although he didn't have much experience, he __was able to__ repair his car.
8. It rained Sunday afternoon, so __we weren't able to__ have a picnic at the park.

Written Exercise (p. 46)

1. The doctor says __our baby sister will be able to walk__ in a couple of months.
2. Her mother says __she'll be able to wear makeup__ when she's fourteen.
3. Her mother says __she'll be able to go out with boys__ when she's in high school.
4. The coach says __he'll be able to play on the football team__ when he's a little bigger.
5. Mr. Bascomb says __she'll be able to take her vacation__ in July.
6. Mr. Golo says __they'll be able to buy a new house__ next year.
7. His boss says __Mr. Green will be able to retire__ in three years.

8. Her father says __she'll be able to travel__ when she's a little older.
9. He says __we'll be able to use our washing machine__ tomorrow.
10. His secretary says __he'll be able to make a decision__ in a few days.

Written Exercise (p. 48)

1. My sister loves to cook. She __may open__ a restaurant someday.
2. She doesn't enjoy living in Los Angeles. She __may move__ to New York.
3. Stanley is worried. He __may lose__ his job at the post office.
4. He can't read small print as well as he used to. He __may need__ glasses.
5. Jenny is a very good student. She __may be__ the best student in her class.
6. Roger __may think__ he's the best student, but he isn't.
7. It's getting cloudy. It __may rain__ today.
8. Mr. Farley is getting tired of waiting for his wife. He __may leave__ without her.
9. We're having problems with our car. We __may sell__ it and get a new one.
10. Gloria wants to study Italian. She __may visit__ Rome next year.

Pair Work (p. 48)

Answers will vary.

1. A: Do you think Nancy will leave the hospital this weekend?
   B: I don't know. She might stay another day.
2. A: Are Jimmy and Linda going to study in the library?
   B: I don't know. They might study in the cafeteria.
3. A: Are they going to walk home?
   B: I don't know. They might take the bus.
4. A: Do you think there will be a meeting on Friday?
   B: I don't know. There might be a meeting.
5. A: Do you think it's a good idea to build a toy factory in City Park?
   B: I don't know. It might be a bad idea.
6. A: Are you going to vote for Mr. Bascomb?
   B: I don't know. I might vote for him.
7. A: Do you think he'll win the election?
   B: I don't know. He might win.

Written Exercise (p. 50)

1. That man is very tall. He __looks like__ a basketball player.
2. I like the way he talks. He __sounds like__ an actor.
3. It's very cold outside. It __feels like__ winter.
4. This soup is delicious. It __tastes like__ homemade soup.

5. We've heard a lot about your sister. She ___sounds like___ a nice person.
6. I like this shampoo. It ___smells like___ lemons.
7. This bed is really hard. It ___feels like___ a rock.
8. Barbara is very pretty. She ___looks like___ a movie star.
9. With her soft voice, she ___sounds like___ Marilyn Monroe.
10. Have you just taken a shower? You ___smell like___ soap.
11. This is the best hamburger I've ever eaten. It ___tastes like___ steak.
12. Your car is very comfortable. It ___feels like___ a Mercedes.

Free Response (p. 50)
Answers will vary.

Story Questions (p. 53)
Answers may vary.

1. The cost of medical care is very high.
2. Health insurance pays at least part of one's medical expenses.
3. There are millions of Americans who have no health insurance because they are unemployed and can't afford it, or their companies don't provide it.
4. Many poor people don't get regular checkups because they don't have health insurance and they can't afford it.
5. When they get sick, the state ends up paying for it.
6. They eat too many foods that are high in cholesterol, such as meat and dairy products, and not enough fresh fruit and vegetables. Moreover, Americans have too much stress in their lives, and they don't get enough exercise.
7. At Frampton Hospital, the doctors try to help their patients by giving them advice on exercise and nutrition.
8. Maria Miranda is popular because she is very kind to her patients and gives them lots of attention.
9. Nancy Paine has been at the hospital for five days.
10. Nancy's friends brought her some nice presents. They brought her flowers, photographs, chocolates, and some magazines and a book.
11. Nancy's only regret is that she's not able to help Otis any more with his campaign for mayor.
12. No, she won't be able to fly her plane again for quite a while.
13. She's worried about her insurance because it only covers the first week in the hospital.
14. According to Nancy, the hospital food tastes awful.
15. Yes. Maria is going to ask Tino to bring Nancy some food from the restaurant.

Talking about Health Care (p. 53)
Answers may vary.

Pair Work 1 (p. 53)
Answers will vary.

Pair Work 2 (p. 53)
Answers will vary.

1. A: Linda wants to learn how to sew.
   B: If she takes lessons, she'll be able to sew in a few months.
2. A: Fred wants to learn how to dance.
   B: If he takes lessons, he'll be able to dance in a few months.
3. A: Jenny wants to learn how to swim.
   B: If she takes lessons, she'll be able to swim in a few months.
4. A: Albert wants to learn how to ski.
   B: If he takes lessons, he'll be able to ski in a few winters.
5. A: Peter wants to learn how to play tennis.
   B: If he takes lessons, he'll be able to play tennis in a few months.
6. A: Anne wants to learn how to drive a car.
   B: If she takes lessons, she'll be able to drive a car in a few months.
7. A: Johnnie wants to learn how to speak Spanish.
   B: If he takes lessons, he'll be able to speak Spanish in a few years.
8. A: Maria wants to learn how to play the guitar.
   B: If she takes lessons, she'll be able to play the guitar in a few weeks.

Practice (p. 54)
1. Peter loves to go out with beautiful women. But if he gets married, he won't be able to go out with beautiful women (except his wife!) any more.
2. Mr. and Mrs. Brown love to work in the garden. But if they sell their house, they won't be able to work in the garden any more.
3. Otis loves to spend his afternoons in the park. But if he becomes mayor, he won't be able to spend his afternoons in the park any more.
4. Jimmy and Linda love to have noisy parties. But if the neighbors complain too much, they won't be able to have noisy parties any more.
5. Jenny loves to wear her old jeans. But if she keeps growing, she won't be able to wear her old jeans any more.
6. Fred loves to get up at noon. But if he takes a job at the post office, he won't be able to get up at noon any more.
7. We love to play tennis. But if they close the park, we won't be able to play tennis any more.
8. Mr. Golo loves to work at home. But if his wife complains too much, he won't be able to work at home any more.

9. He loves to drive a big car. But if gasoline becomes too expensive, he won't be able to drive a big car any more.

Pair Work (p. 54)
Answers will vary.

Written Exercise (p. 55)
Answers will vary.

1. Don't try to read in bad light. You might hurt your eyes.
2. Don't forget your umbrella. It might rain.
3. Don't eat too much cake. You might get fatter.
4. Don't drive too fast. You might get into an accident.
5. Don't pull the dog's tail. He might bite you.
6. Don't play football in your white pants. They might get dirty.
7. Don't criticize Gladys. She might feel bad.
8. Don't play the piano after midnight. The neighbors might complain.

"Money" Questions (p. 57)
Answers may vary.

1. Money is important because people need it to live. They use money to pay for food, clothes, housing, transportation—everything they need for survival.
2. Honest people work hard for their money.
3. Con artists make money selling worthless goods. They know that it's easy to separate fools from their money, and they are always finding new ways to do it.
4. People say that "love of money is the root of all evil" because most crimes involve money.

(Answers will vary.) I disagree, because many crimes involve love.

5. Abraham Lincoln was a president of the United States. Before that, he worked in a general store. He got the name "Honest Abe" because of his very honest deeds.
6. A big spender is often very generous and likes to buy expensive presents for his or her friends. A cheapskate is always looking for bargains and hardly ever spends money on other people.
7. Answers will vary. Yes, big spenders have more fun than cheapskates, because they spend less time worrying about money.
8. "Money doesn't grow on trees" means that it's not easy to get money.
9. "Nobody knows when you're down and out" means that other people will be unaware of your difficulties. (Answers will vary.) I don't think it's true, because friends and family stand by each other.

Free Response (p. 57)
Answers will vary.

Test (p. 58)

1. B	3. D	5. B	7. C	9. B
2. C	4. B	6. B	8. A	10. D

Free Response (p. 58)
Answers will vary.

Talking about Sports, Group Work, Talking about Friendship, Group Work, and Talking about Health Care (p. 59)
Answers will vary.

WORKBOOK EXERCISES

▶ANSWERS

Exercise 1 (p. 21)
1. Will she be able to clean the house tomorrow?
2. Will he be able to play football tomorrow?
3. Will she be able to finish her work tomorrow?
4. Will he be able to pick up the package tomorrow?
5. Will she be able to do the wash tomorrow?
6. Will he be able to see the doctor tomorrow?
7. Will she be able to receive visitors tomorrow?
8. Will he be able to drive his car tomorrow?
9. Will she be able to go to school tomorrow?
10. Will she be able to take the test tomorrow?

Exercise 2 (p. 22)
1. He wasn't able to sleep.
2. He wasn't able to see the movie.
3. She wasn't able to play the guitar.
4. He wasn't able to wash the dishes.
5. She wasn't able to reach the cookies.
6. He wasn't able to read the newspaper.
7. She wasn't able to carry the suitcase.
8. He wasn't able to get a haircut.

Exercise 3 (p. 23)
Answers will vary.

Exercise 4 (p. 23)
1. She sounds French.
2. It smells good.
3. It tastes awful.
4. I feel sick.
5. It sounds fabulous.
6. It looks terrible.
7. She smells nice.
8. It feels hard.
9. It looks expensive.
10. It tastes delicious.

Exercise 5 (p. 24)
Answers will vary.

Exercise 6 (p. 25)
Answers will vary.

Exercise 7 (p. 26)

Barney:	Hi, Joe. How are you doing?
Joe:	Not too good. Business is/has been very slow.
Barney:	I'm sorry to hear that.
Joe:	I've been losing customers ever since they opened that joint down the street.
Barney:	What joint are you talking about? You mean Mom's Cafe?
Joe:	Yeah. You know the place?
Barney:	Sure. Everybody knows Mom's. It's a great place to eat.
Joe:	What's so great about it? What do they have that I don't?
Barney:	Well, for one thing, they serve good food. Have you ever tried Mom's meatloaf? It's delicious. Mom makes the best—
Joe:	Okay, I've heard enough. Please don't mention Mom's any more. I get a headache every time I hear that name.
Barney:	Sorry, Joe. I promise I'll never mention her name again.
Joe:	You're a pal. Would you like a cup of coffee?
Barney:	No, thanks. I've got to run.
Joe:	Where are you going?
Barney:	To meet Nancy. We're having lunch at that joint down the street.

Exercise 8 (p. 27)
1. He has a lot of bad habits.
2. I didn't get much sleep last night.
3. I'm having trouble making a decision.
4. Can you use your influence to help me get a job at the bank?
5. I'm sure I can do well if they just give me a chance.
6. He has no ambition.
7. She has a beautiful voice.
8. Movies and concerts are my favorite kinds of entertainment.
9. They gave a great performance.
10. I don't give compliments very often, but I think you have a beautiful smile.

Exercise 9 (p. 27)
Answers will vary.

Exercise 10 (p. 28)
Composition

CHAPTER 4

► **ANSWERS**

Story Questions (p. 66)

1. He was a dirty, little man.
2. Mr. Bascomb gave the man one dollar the first time.
3. He went back a second time to give more money because he felt sorry for the man. He could not imagine not eating for a whole day.
4. Mr. Bascomb had a clever idea. He offered to buy lunch for the man.
5. The man said that the restaurant would not permit someone like him to enter such a fine restaurant.
6. The man ordered milk for lunch.
7. Mr. Bascomb ordered more food because he understood that the man had already eaten.
8. He ran toward the door because he didn't want to pay for the lunch.
9. The man finally paid for the meal.
10. He probably tried to get back the tip from the waiter.
11. Answers will vary. Mr. Bascomb is sensitive, because he pitied the man. He is perceptive, because he realized that the man was lying. He values honesty, because he forced the man to be honest. I do/don't admire him because the poor man was poor, which is pitiful regardless of his dishonesty.
12. Answers will vary.

Written Exercise (p. 66)

1. Johnnie missed the bus. _So did_ Anne.
2. They're always late. _So are_ you.
3. We didn't go to the football game. _Neither did_ they.
4. She lives on a quiet street. _So does_ he.
5. He won't get paid this week. _Neither will_ she.
6. They've been wasting a lot of time. _So have_ we.
7. I don't like to get up early. _Neither does_ Fred.
8. He isn't very ambitious. _Neither is_ Barney.
9. We can do a better job. _So can_ they.
10. They won't be home Saturday. _Neither will_ I.

Pair Work (p. 66)

Answers will vary.

1. A: Have you ever walked in the rain?
   B: Yes, I have. I walked in the rain last night.
      or No, I haven't. But I've walked in the snow.
2. A: Have you ever caught a butterfly?
   B: Yes, I have. I caught one last summer.
      or No, I haven't. But I've caught a grasshopper.

3. A: Have you ever climbed a mountain?
   B: Yes, I have. I climb mountains every summer.
      or No, I haven't. But I've been hiking.
4. A: Have you ever slept under the stars?
   B: Yes, I have. I slept under the stars when I was camping.
      or No, I haven't. I don't like to sleep outside.
5. A: Have you ever taken a cold shower?
   B: Yes, I have. I took a cold shower this morning!
      or No, I haven't. A cold shower will make you sick!
6. A: Have you ever gotten a bad haircut?
   B: Yes, I have. In fact, my last haircut was terrible.
      or No, I haven't. My wife is a great hair-cutter.
7. A: Have you ever met a famous person?
   B: Yes, I have. I met Ronald McDonald at his restaurant.
      or No, I haven't. But once I saw Michael Jordan on a street corner.
8. A: Have you ever done something crazy?
   B: Yes, I have. I took a walk in the snow with no shoes on.
      or No, I haven't. My life is pretty boring.
9. A: Have you ever broken anything?
   B: Yes, I have. I broke my left leg when I was young.
      or No, I haven't. I'm always careful.
10. A: Have you ever had a car accident?
    B: Yes, I have. I didn't stop at a stop sign and I hit another car.
       or No, I haven't. In fact, I don't drive.
11. A: Have you ever lost something valuable?
    B: Yes, I have. I lost my mother's favorite necklace.
       or No, I haven't. I've only lost small things.
12. A: Have you ever helped a stranger?
    B: Yes, I have. In fact, I helped a foreigner find the post office yesterday.
       or No, I haven't. I'm too shy to talk to strangers.

Pair Work (p. 67)

1. A: Does Ed watch as _much_ television as Johnnie?
   B: Yes, he does. He watches _more_ television than Johnnie.
2. A: Does Barbara make as _many_ mistakes as Anne?
   B: No, she doesn't. Anne makes _more_ mistakes than Barbara.

3. A: Does Ula Hackey spend as __much__ money as Betty?
   B: Yes, she does. She spends more money than Betty.
4. A: Does Jack have as __many__ problems as Mr. Farley?
   B: No, he doesn't. Mr. Farley has more problems than Jack.
5. A: Does Anne drink as __much__ coffee as Johnnie?
   B: No, she doesn't. Johnnie drinks more coffee than Anne.
6. A: Does Otis eat as __many__ vegetables as Gloria?
   B: Yes, he does. He eats more vegetables than Gloria.
7. A: Does Jenny read as __many__ comic books as Marty?
   B: No, she doesn't. Marty reads more comic books than Jenny.
8. A: Does Fred sleep as __much__ as Mr. Bascomb?
   B: Yes, he does. He sleeps more than Mr. Bascomb.

Pair Work, Group Work, Discussion, and Pair Work (p. 70)
Answers will vary.

Pair Work (p. 71)
Answers will vary.

Talking about Dating (p. 72)
Answers will vary.

Written Exercise (p. 72)
1. Sam was tired when he got home, __so__ he took a rest.
2. Mabel has stopped eating dessert __in order to__ lose weight.
3. We decided to watch TV __since__ we had nothing better to do.
4. You won't be able to finish that job __unless__ you get some help.
5. Mr. Poole likes sports __although__ he isn't a very good athlete.
6. He takes the bus to work __in order to__ save money.
7. His wife doesn't like her job __although__ the pay is very good.
8. They will take their vacation next week __unless__ something happens.
9. Linda wasn't having a good time at the party, __so__ she left early.
10. Albert didn't go to the party __since__ he wasn't feeling well.

Practice (p. 72)
1. Where has he been spending his afternoons?
2. What has he been reading?
3. Who has he been avoiding?
4. What has she been trying to find out?
5. Where has she been going?
6. Who has she been talking to?
7. What have they been telling her?
8. Who has she been trying to see?
9. Where have they been staying?

Pair Work (p. 73)
Answers may vary.

1. A: Have you been going out a lot?
   B: Yes, I have. I've been going out every night.
   or No, I haven't. I don't like going out.
2. A: Have you been meeting a lot of people?
   B: Yes, I have. I've been meeting new people every day.
   or No, I haven't. I've been staying at home a lot lately.
3. A: Have you been spending a lot of money?
   B: Yes, I have. I've been spending more than I make.
   or No, I haven't. I've been trying to save.
4. A: Have you been working hard?
   B: Yes, I have. I've been working a lot lately.
   or No, I haven't. I haven't been working much lately.
5. A: Have you been getting a lot of exercise?
   B: Yes, I have. I've been exercising every afternoon.
   or No, I haven't. I've been watching TV a lot lately.
6. A: Have you been watching TV a lot?
   B: Yes, I have. I've been watching TV every night.
   or No, I haven't. I've been going to the movies a lot lately.
7. A: Have you been going to bed late?
   B: Yes, I have. I've been going to bed every night after midnight.
   or No, I haven't. I've been going to bed early this week.
8. A: Have you been getting enough sleep?
   B: Yes, I have. I've been getting more than enough sleep.
   or No, I haven't. I never get enough sleep.

Practice (p. 73)
1. I wonder whose camera he borrowed.
2. I wonder who he gave the photographs to.
3. I wonder where she went.
4. I wonder whose car she drove.
5. I wonder who he called.
6. I wonder where they had dinner.
7. I wonder whose party they went to.
8. I wonder who she made a date with.
9. I wonder where they studied.

Written Exercise (p. 73)
Answers will vary.

Written Exercise (p. 74)

1. The boy <u>whose</u> team lost the football game was very unhappy.
2. He talked so fast I couldn't understand <u>what</u> he was saying.
3. The woman <u>who</u> lives in that house has a lot of valuable paintings.
4. I don't know <u>why</u> she never told you about her paintings.
5. This pen isn't mine. I wonder <u>whose</u> pen it is.
6. Please close the door <u>when</u> you leave the room.
7. Did you hear about <u>what</u> happened last night?
8. Someone robbed the store <u>where</u> my sister works.
9. She saw the man <u>who</u> took the money.
10. She was afraid. That's <u>why</u> she didn't call the police.
11. The robber turned off the lights <u>when</u> he left the store.
12. Nobody knows <u>where</u> he went.

Pair Work (p. 74)

1. A: The Golos sold their house last week.
   B: No, they didn't.
2. A: They're going to live in Canada.
   B: No, they aren't.
3. A: The bank was closed yesterday.
   B: No, it wasn't.
4. A: Mr. Bascomb didn't go to work.
   B: Yes, he did.
5. A: He doesn't like his job.
   B: Yes, he does.
6. A: He's very lazy.
   B: No, he isn't.
7. A: Jenny has been watching TV all day.
   B: No, she hasn't.
8. A: She hasn't done her homework yet.
   B: Yes, she has.
9. A: She isn't a very good student.
   B: Yes, she is.
10. A: She gets poor grades in school.
    B: No, she doesn't.
11. A: We can't see our friends tonight.
    B: Yes, we can.
12. A: We won't have enough time.
    B: Yes, we will.

Problem Solving (p. 75)
Answers will vary.

Getting the Details (p. 75)
Answers will vary.

Pair Work (p. 76)

1. A: Vote for me!
   B: Why? Give me one good reason.
   A: If you elect me, I'll save City Park.
   B: Sounds good. You have my vote.
   or Hmm . . . I'll have to think about it.
   or You must be joking.
   or I don't believe you.
2. A: Vote for me!
   B: Why? Give me one good reason.
   A: If you elect me, I'll feed the hungry.
   B: Sounds good. You have my vote.
   or Hmm . . . I'll have to think about it.
   or You must be joking.
   or I don't believe you.
3. A: Vote for me!
   B: Why? Give me one good reason.
   A: If you elect me, I'll create new jobs.
   B: Sounds good. You have my vote.
   or Hmm . . . I'll have to think about it.
   or You must be joking.
   or I don't believe you.
4. A: Vote for me!
   B: Why? Give me one good reason.
   A: If you elect me, I'll make the streets safe.
   B: Sounds good. You have my vote.
   or Hmm . . . I'll have to think about it.
   or You must be joking.
   or I don't believe you.
5. A: Vote for me!
   B: Why? Give me one good reason.
   A: If you elect me, I'll put the criminals in jail.
   B: Sounds good. You have my vote.
   or Hmm . . . I'll have to think about it.
   or You must be joking.
   or I don't believe you.
6. A: Vote for me!
   B: Why? Give me one good reason.
   A: If you elect me, I'll improve transportation.
   B: Sounds good. You have my vote.
   or Hmm . . . I'll have to think about it.
   or You must be joking.
   or I don't believe you.
7. A: Vote for me!
   B: Why? Give me one good reason.
   A: If you elect me, I'll eliminate pollution.
   B: Sounds good. You have my vote.
   or Hmm . . . I'll have to think about it.
   or You must be joking.
   or I don't believe you.
8. A: Vote for me!
   B: Why? Give me one good reason.
   A: If you elect me, I'll build more schools.
   B: Sounds good. You have my vote.
   or Hmm . . . I'll have to think about it.
   or You must be joking.
   or I don't believe you.
9. A: Vote for me!
   B: Why? Give me one good reason.
   A: If you elect me, I'll provide better health care.
   B: Sounds good. You have my vote.

or Hmm . . . I'll have to think about it.

or You must be joking.

or I don't believe you.

Talking about Politics (p. 77)

Answers will vary.

Written Exercise (p. 77)

1. Come here. There's <u>something</u> I have to tell you.
2. My sister didn't give me <u>anything</u> for my birthday.
3. She's busy now. She's talking to <u>someone</u> on the phone.
4. We stayed home last night. We didn't go <u>anywhere</u>.
5. I've never met <u>anyone</u> like Mr. Poole.
6. He can't do <u>anything</u> right.
7. That woman looks familiar. I've seen her <u>somewhere</u> before.
8. She's lonely. She needs <u>someone</u> to talk to.
9. I've lost my watch! I can't find it <u>anywhere</u>.
10. Has <u>anyone</u> seen my gold watch?

11. If you're hungry, we can get <u>something</u> to eat at Joe's Cafe.
12. I don't like Joe's Cafe. Let's go <u>somewhere</u> else.

Pair Work (p. 77)

Answers will vary.

Free Response (p. 78)

Answers will vary.

Test (pp. 79–81)

1. B	14. B	27. A	39. B
2. C	15. D	28. C	40. D
3. A	16. B	29. B	41. C
4. D	17. A	30. A	42. A
5. B	18. A	31. C	43. B
6. D	19. B	32. C	44. C
7. A	20. D	33. B	45. D
8. B	21. C	34. D	46. A
9. A	22. D	35. D	47. D
10. B	23. A	36. A	48. C
11. C	24. D	37. A	49. D
12. D	25. B	38. C	50. A
13. C	26. C		

WORKBOOK EXERCISES

▶ ANSWERS

Exercise 1 (pp. 31–32)

1. They're going to sweep the sidewalk.
   They're sweeping the sidewalk.
   They've just swept the sidewalk.
2. He's going to shave.
   He's shaving.
   He's just shaved.
3. They're going to wash the car.
   They're washing the car.
   They've just washed the car.
4. She's going to take a shower.
   She's taking a shower.
   She's just taken a shower.
5. They're going to paint the room.
   They're painting the room.
   They've just painted the room.
6. He's going to buy some flowers.
   He's buying some flowers.
   He's just bought some flowers.

Exercise 2 (p. 33)

1. Do you have any idea where Nancy went?
2. I wonder when she will be back.
3. Do you know where Peter works?
4. Could you tell me how much he makes?
5. Give me one good reason why I should tell you.
6. I don't understand what this word means.
7. Do you know where the dictionary is?
8. I wonder why Gloria got upset.
9. Can you tell me how she lost her keys?
10. Show me which photograph you like best.

Exercise 3 (p. 33)

1. When John arrived, the party was over.
2. It was so dark we couldn't see anything.
3. Do you know what time it is?
4. I wonder when they will come home.
5. Neither of them likes cold weather. *or* Both of them dislike cold weather.
6. That's the woman whose cat ate my canary.
7. She looks terrible in that dress.
8. Fred sings worse than Barney.
9. How many people live in that house?
10. Only Gloria and I know the answer.

Exercise 4 (p. 34)

1. Maria bought a hat and a coat. The hat was cheap, but the coat was expensive.
2. Peter has a problem. He can't find the key to his office.
3. I saw the woman you were talking to me about. She has a beautiful smile.
4. Have you ever been to Mom's Cafe? It's a very good place to eat. The food is excellent.
5. I love coffee. It's the best drink in the world. I'm going to have a cup of coffee right now.
6. Let's go to a movie. There's a good one playing at the Rex Theater on Main Street. The first show starts at six.
7. What a beautiful house! Do you know the people who live there?
8. We have a color television and a black and white television. The color television is upstairs and the black and white is downstairs.
9. California has beautiful mountains, but I like the ocean better. I love to go swimming on a sunny day.

Exercise 5 (p. 35)

1. Tomorrow, July 9, is Tony's birthday. You forgot, didn't you?
2. Unfortunately, we were in a hurry and didn't have time to call you.
3. When I get home, I'm going to take off my shoes, lie down, and relax.
4. Listen, you have to work hard if you want to be successful.
5. My cousin, Janet Warner, works in a hotel on the west side of town.
6. Her boyfriend is tall, dark, and handsome, but he has no ambition.

Exercise 6 (p. 36)

1. Last Saturday, I went to a movie with Jane.
2. Did you see the play *Death of a Salesman*?
3. Robert Palmer, the famous actor, lives in New York.
4. Nancy learned to speak Spanish when she was in Mexico.
5. My brother likes to go to the mountains in the winter.
6. Our neighbor works at the post office on Main Street.
7. The next meeting of the Lions Club is on Friday, April 22.

Exercise 7 (p. 37)

1. I have been waiting for you for over an hour.
2. You have been eating too much bread.
3. She has been working at the office all day.
4. We have been spending a lot of time there recently.
5. He has been driving since he was sixteen.
6. My neighbors have been playing loud music all afternoon.
7. His company has been making a lot of money recently.
8. He has been studying it for five years.
9. He has been living with an American family in New York for the last six months.
10. He has been thinking (talking) about them a lot recently.

Exercise 8 (p. 37)

1. You're coming to the meeting, aren't you?
2. You won't forget, will you?
3. You know Barney, don't you?
4. He didn't call last night, did he?
5. He was working, wasn't he?
6. He couldn't leave his job, could he?
7. You'd like to talk to Gloria, wouldn't you?
8. You haven't seen her today, have you?
9. You don't have her number, do you?
10. You lost it, didn't you?

Exercise 9 (p. 38)
Composition

►PRELIMINARY ORAL WORK

Will Have to/Had to (pp. 83–86)

Have to is similar in meaning to *must* and provides an alternative form for the present and future tenses:

> He must see the doctor. = He has to see the doctor.
> He must see the doctor next week. = He will have to see the doctor next week.

Must cannot be used in the past tense; we use *had to* to indicate past time:

> She had to work last Saturday.

Have students make sentences using *had to:*

> Teacher: Yesterday I had to clean my apartment. Tell me something you had to do yesterday.
> Student: Yesterday I had to make dinner for my family.

Have students complete sentences of the type given below using *will have to:*

> If you want to see the doctor, you'll have to make an appointment.

> If you want to be successful, . . .
> If you want to send a package, . . .
> If you want to borrow money, . . .
> If you want to pass the test, . . .
> If you want to be a good tennis player, . . .
> If you want to lose weight, . . .
> If you want to be healthy, . . .
> If you want your car to stay in good condition, . . .
> If you want your plants to grow, . . .
> If you want people to be nice to you, . . .
> If you want to learn how to play the guitar, . . .

Verb + Object + Infinitive (with *to*) (pp. 87–90)

Verbs like *want, ask, tell, invite,* etc. are often used with object + infinitive (with *to*):

> She wants him to paint the kitchen.
> They invited me to come to the party.

See page 162 in the appendix for a list of verbs that are followed by object + infinitive (with *to*).

Have students make sentences using verb + object + infinitive (with *to*):

> Teacher: Sam told his children, Jimmy and Linda, to help with the housework. He gave them several jobs to do. What did he want them to do?

> wash the dishes
> He wanted them to wash the dishes.

> clean the windows

> Student: He wanted them to clean the windows.

> Teacher: take out the trash
> sweep the sidewalk
> rake the leaves
> cut the grass
> water the plants
> wash the car
> vacuum the living room
> polish the furniture
> wax the floor

> Teacher: Tell me what your friends and family want you to do.
> Student: My brother wants me to give a party.
> Teacher: Tell me what you want other people to do.
> Student: I want Maria to give me her phone number.

Introduce other verbs that are followed by object + infinitive (with *to*): *ask, tell, invite, expect, help, pay.*

Would Rather

Would rather means *prefer* and can only be followed by an infinitive (without *to*):

> Would you like an apple for lunch?
> No, I'd rather have an orange.

> Would you rather read a book or watch TV?
> I'd rather read a book.

Ask students questions using *would rather:*

> Teacher: Would you rather go to a movie or play a sport?
> Student: I'd rather play a sport.

Supposed to

This idiom expresses an obligation or duty, similar in meaning to *must,* but not as strong:

> You're supposed to wash the dishes.
> He's supposed to take care of the dog.

Supposed to can also express an assumption, something that is thought to be true:

> She's supposed to be a good dancer.
> He's supposed to have a lot of money.

Have students tell what they are supposed to do at home, at school, at work, etc.

CHAPTER 5

▶ANSWERS

Reading (p. 84)
1. Sam and Jack often talk about their days in the army.
2. Yes, they had to get up early in the morning.
3. They had to march at least ten miles a day.
4. They had to do without television and computer games.
5. They only made about $80 a month.
6. The army paid their expenses.
7. They had very little freedom in the beginning.
8. After the first six weeks, they didn't have to stay at the base all the time.
9. Jack didn't like being in the army, since he didn't like taking orders.
10. Sam didn't complain because he thought being in the army was a good experience, and that everyone should serve their country.

Pair Work (p. 84)
Answers will vary.

1. A: Jack doesn't like to work hard, does he?
   B: No, but he had to work hard when he was in the army.
2. A: Jack doesn't like to exercise, does he?
   B: No, but he had to march at least ten miles a day when he was in the army.
3. A: Jack doesn't like to shave every day, does he?
   B: No, but he probably had to shave every day when he was in the army.
4. A: Jack doesn't like to shine his shoes, does he?
   B: No, but he probably had to shine his shoes every day when he was in the army.
5. A: Jack doesn't like to make his bed, does he?
   B: No, but he probably had to make his bed every day when he was in the army.
6. A: Jack doesn't like to wear heavy boots, does he?
   B: No, but he probably had to wear heavy boots every day when he was in the army.
7. A: Jack doesn't like to take orders, does he?
   B: No, but he probably had to take orders every day when he was in the army.
8. A: Jack doesn't like to attend a lot of meetings, does he?
   B: No, but he probably had to attend a lot of meetings when he was in the army.
9. A: Jack doesn't like to hurry, does he?
   B: No, but he probably had to hurry a lot when he was in the army.

Pair Work (p. 86)
1. A: Albert wants to lose weight, but he doesn't like to exercise.
   B: If he wants to lose weight, he'll have to exercise.
2. A: Linda wants to be a good tennis player, but she doesn't like to practice.
   B: If she wants to be a good tennis player, she'll have to practice.
3. A: Anne wants to learn Spanish, but she doesn't like to study.
   B: If she wants to learn Spanish, she'll have to study.
4. A: Peter wants to go fishing with Tino, but he doesn't like to get up early.
   B: If he wants to go fishing with Tino, he'll have to get up early.
5. A: My sister wants to go to college, but she doesn't like to study.
   B: If she wants to go to college, she'll have to study.
6. A: Jack wants to be a success, but he doesn't like to work hard.
   B: If he wants to be a success, he'll have to work hard.
7. A: Sandy wants to save money, but she doesn't like to eat in cheap restaurants.
   B: If she wants to save money, she'll have to eat in cheap restaurants.
8. A: Barney wants to look good, but he doesn't like to iron his clothes.
   B: If he wants to look good, he'll have to iron his clothes.
9. A: Mabel wants to please her husband, but she doesn't like to cook Chinese food.
   B: If she wants to please her husband, she'll have to cook Chinese food.
10. A: Mr. Poole wants to please his wife, but he doesn't like to go to the opera.
    B: If he wants to please his wife, he'll have to go to the opera.

Practice (p. 86)
1. You won't have to attend them.
2. You won't have to call her.
3. You won't have to show her.
4. You won't have to repair it.
5. You won't have to clean it.
6. You won't have to help him.
7. You won't have to take me.
8. You won't have to wake me up.
9. You won't have to tell them.
10. You won't have to show them.

Reading (p. 88)
1. Fred used to play professional baseball.
2. Everyone expected him to take a job at his father's ice cream factory.
3. Fred would rather eat ice cream than sell it.
4. Once he tried working for an insurance company downtown.

5. He was supposed to be on the job at 8:30 in the morning, but that was too early for Fred.
6. Now Fred spends most of his time in the park.
7. He teaches boys how to play baseball.
8. Whenever Fred needs a little money, he sells hot dogs at the sports stadium.
9. Mona wants him to get a regular job.
10. Last week she sent him to see a man at the Ace Employment Company.
11. She told Fred to wear a suit and tie for the interview.
12. She reminded him to be polite because she wanted him to make a good impression.

Pair Work (p. 88)
1. A: What did they expect him to do—work for his father?
   B: That's right. They expected him to work for his father.
2. A: Where did he invite her to go—to a movie?
   B: That's right. He invited her to go to a movie.
3. A: What did she remind him to take—an umbrella?
   B: That's right. She reminded him to take an umbrella.
4. A: Who did they want us to meet—Mr. Bascomb?
   B: That's right. They wanted us to meet Mr. Bascomb.
5. A: When did he tell us to come—at nine o'clock?
   B: That's right. He told us to come at nine o'clock.
6. A: Where did she expect him to go—to the store?
   B: That's right. She expected him to go to the store.
7. A: What did she ask him to buy—some milk?
   B: That's right. She asked him to buy some milk.
8. A: What did they tell us to bring—some hot dogs?
   B: That's right. They told us to bring some hot dogs.

Pair Work (p. 90)
1. A: Did Sam go to the market?
   B: I think so. Mabel asked him to go to the market.
2. A: Will the neighbors bring some food?
   B: I hope so. We reminded them to bring some food.
3. A: Will Linda clean the kitchen?
   B: Yes. I told her to clean the kitchen.
4. A: Will Jimmy help her?
   B: He should. We asked him to help her.
5. A: Did Albert pick up the package?
   B: I hope so. We sent him to pick up the package.

6. A: Did Jenny go to the party?
   B: Yes. Her mother allowed her to go to the party.
7. A: Is she learning how to play the piano?
   B: That's right. Ms. Finch is teaching her how to play the piano.
8. A: Will Peter come over tomorrow?
   B: I hope so. We invited him to come over tomorrow.
9. A: Did he call the hospital?
   B: I think so. Maria asked him to call the hospital.
10. A: Did they find the keys?
    B: Yes. We helped them find the keys.

Story Questions (p. 91)
Answers may vary.

1. It has friendly people, sunny weather, and many outstanding tourist attractions.
2. The city is close to the mountains, and it's only a few miles from the Pacific Ocean. There is good skiing in the wintertime, and during the summer months people enjoy camping and fishing at Bear Lake. The Pacific coastline is very beautiful. At the beach, you can play volleyball, swim in the ocean, or just relax and read a good book. Everyone has a great time.
3. Wickam City has only a few first-class hotels. They can't begin to accommodate all the people who would like to stay there.

Story Questions (p. 92)
Answers may vary.

1. Peter and Maria got in Peter's sports car and drove to Sunset Beach.
2. I don't think Maria enjoys the beach as much as Peter does, because she complained.
3. When Maria saw Otis and Gloria, Maria wanted to exchange the car for the bicycles.
4. They all agreed to meet at the beach and have lunch together at the Seahorse Restaurant.
5. Peter didn't enjoy riding a bicycle because he was hot and sweaty, and his legs ached.
6. Otis said that he was never going to drive a car again.
7. First the car ran out of gas, then the motor stopped, and finally it had a flat tire.
8. He had to walk a mile to get gas, fix the motor, and change the tire.
9. Answers will vary. Otis and Peter learned that "the grass is always greener on the other side."

Free Response (p. 93)
Answers will vary.

Pair Work (p. 93)
1. A: Would you rather sing or dance?
   B: I'd rather sing.
   or I'd rather dance.
   or I like both.

2. A: Would you rather go to a movie or see a play?
   B: I'd rather go to a movie.
      or I'd rather see a play.
      or I like both.
3. A: Would you rather study at home or in the library?
   B: I'd rather study at home.
      or I'd rather study in the library.
      or I like both.
4. A: Would you rather listen to classical music or rock?
   B: I'd rather listen to classical music.
      or I'd rather listen to rock.
      or I like both.
5. A: Would you rather talk about sports or politics?
   B: I'd rather talk about sports.
      or I'd rather talk about politics.
      or I like both.
6. A: Would you rather work in an office or outdoors?
   B: I'd rather work in an office.
      or I'd rather work outdoors.
      or I like both.
7. A: Would you rather have a lot of money or a lot of friends?
   B: I'd rather have a lot of money.
      or I'd rather have a lot of friends.
      or I like both.
8. A: Would you rather live in the city or in the country?
   B: I'd rather live in the city.
      or I'd rather live in the country.
      or I like both.

Practice (p. 93)
1. He's too lazy to do any work.
2. He's too cheap to take his girlfriend to a nice restaurant.
3. She's too sophisticated to eat with her fingers.
4. She's too nice to tell her boyfriend he has bad taste.
5. He's too proud to ask her for money.
6. She's too upset to eat her dinner.
7. He's too nervous to talk in front of a big crowd.
8. She's too frightened to walk home alone.

Written Exercise (p. 94)
1. Please be quiet. You're __making__ too much noise.
2. The girls are __doing__ their homework.
3. Mabel __did__ the cleaning yesterday.
4. Sam __made__ $80 a month when he was in the army.
5. Linda always __does__ her best to __make__ a good impression.
6. Nancy was happy that she could __do__ something to help Otis.
7. Have you __done__ the shopping?
8. Mrs. Hamby is going to __make__ sandwiches for lunch.
9. I'm __making__ plans for the future.

10. We hope to __do__ a lot of business in New York.
11. Mr. Bascomb has __made__ several speeches this week.
12. He can't __do__ anything without our support.

Practice (p. 94)
Answers will vary.

1. She wants him to find a regular job.
2. She wants him to wash his dishes.
3. He wants her to lose some weight.
4. She wants him to slow down.
5. Barney wants them to be quiet.
6. She wants him to get better grades.
7. He wants her to go to the doctor.
8. She wants him to visit her.
9. She wants him to hurry up.
10. She wants him to give her money.

Pair Work (p. 94)
Answers will vary.

"Exercise" Questions (p. 96)
Answers may vary.

1. Exercise develops the body's cardiovascular system and muscles and keeps us fit.
2. Their workouts don't make them sweat enough or breathe hard enough. They don't run far enough or exercise long enough.
3. Aerobic exercise forces the cardiovascular system to work harder and supply more oxygen to the muscles. When the oxygen reaches the muscles, it combines with fuel sources to produce energy.
4. The best aerobic exercise is running.
5. The human animal is the best long-distance runner on the planet.
6. Humans are the best distance runners because we have the most efficient sweat glands in the animal kingdom.
7. Weight-training can make your muscles larger, firmer, and stronger.
8. The most important thing is to take it easy at the beginning. Also, pay attention to form to protect yourself from injury.
9. Weight-training is becoming popular among women because it makes them healthier, stronger, and more energetic, and it gives them a feeling of power.
10. For all-around fitness, there's no sport that can take the place of swimming.
11. Swimming builds up your limbs, heart, and lungs. It improves coordination and strength.
12. They might say that exercise is boring, or that they are too busy.
13. Answers will vary.

Talking about Military Service, Group Work, and Talking about Jobs (p. 97)
Answers will vary.

WORKBOOK EXERCISES

▶**Answers**

Exercise 1 (p. 39)
Answers will vary.

Exercise 2 (p. 39)
Answers will vary.

Exercise 3 (p. 40)
1. He wants them to vote for him.
2. She wants him to get up.
3. He wants her to eat her dinner.
4. She wants him to take a shower.
5. He wants him to do his homework.
6. She wants her to answer the phone.
7. He wants her to turn off the radio.
8. She wants him to bring her the menu.

Exercise 4 (p. 41)
Answers will vary.

Exercise 5 (p. 41)
Answers will vary.

Exercise 6 (p. 42)
1. Mabel is going to make some sandwiches for lunch.
2. She is doing her homework.
3. Can you do me a favor and loan me a dime?
4. I have to make a telephone call.
5. Your friends made a lot of noise at the party last night.
6. They did some things we asked them not to do.
7. Everyone makes mistakes.
8. It will do you good.

9. Mr. Bascomb is doing everything he can to win the election this year.
10. He made five speeches last week.
11. It doesn't make any difference what he says.
12. What has he ever done for Wickam City?

Exercise 7 (p. 42)
1. He's supposed to clean the house.
2. She's supposed to do the shopping.
3. They're supposed to pay the bills.
4. You're supposed to get to work on time.

Exercise 8 (p. 43)
1. She was annoyed because he was eating with his fingers.
2. He was mad because the dog was sleeping on the sofa.
3. She was angry because they were talking in the library.
4. He was upset because she was feeding a monkey.
5. He frowned because Jack was speeding/driving too fast.
6. He was upset because they were swimming in the pond.

Exercise 9 (p. 44)
Answers will vary.

Exercise 10 (p. 44)
Answers will vary.

Exercise 11 (pp. 45–46)
Composition

▶PRELIMINARY ORAL WORK

Second Conditional (pp. 101–104)

This type of conditional clause is used for improbable or unlikely conditions. The verb in the *if*-clause is in the simple past tense; the verb in the main clause is in the conditional tense:

> If you washed your car, it would look better.
> If they went to the party, they'd have a good time.

Although we use the simple past tense in the *if*-clause, the sentences are not past; they refer to the present or future and are sometimes called the past subjunctive. The second conditional is used in the following situations:

a. when we don't expect the action in the *if*-clause to take place:
> If he worked harder, he would make more money (but we don't expect him to work harder).

b. when the *if*-clause represents what is contrary to fact:
> If he had a car, he could drive to work (but he doesn't have a car).

c. when we want to give advice:
> If I were you, I'd stop smoking (but I'm not you).

The past subjunctive is also used after *wish* to indicate an unreal situation:

> I wish I could dance.
> I wish you had a car.

Have students make conditional sentences with *could*:

> She doesn't have a watch. She can't tell the time.
> If she had a watch, she could tell the time.

> He doesn't have a car. He can't drive to work.
> We don't have a television. We can't watch the news.
> She doesn't have any money. She can't go to the movies.
> He doesn't have her phone number. He can't call her.
> We don't have their address. We can't write to them.
> You don't have your umbrella. You can't walk home in the rain.
> He doesn't have his glasses. He can't read the newspaper.
> She doesn't have any time. She can't help him.
> He doesn't have a skill. He can't find a job.
> We don't have any flour. We can't make a cake.

Have students give you advice using the second conditional:

> Teacher: Should I have fried eggs or cereal for breakfast?
> Student: If I were you, I'd have fried eggs for breakfast.

> Should I buy a new hat or a new coat?
> Should I paint the kitchen yellow or white?
> Should I plant tomatoes or carrots in the garden?
> Should I have spaghetti or chicken for dinner?
> Should I walk home or take the bus?
> Should I watch TV or read a book tonight?
> Should I study at home or in the library?
> Should I have a party this week or next week?
> Should I serve sandwiches or pizza to the guests?
> Should I go to the mountains or the beach on my next vacation?

Ask students questions using the second conditional:

> Teacher: What would you do if someone gave you a million dollars?
> Student: If someone gave me a million dollars, I'd quit my job/buy a house/travel around the world, etc.

> What would you do if
> . . . you got lost in a strange city?
> . . . a thief took your wallet?
> . . . you saw an automobile accident?
> . . . you had more free time?
> . . . you had a bigger apartment?
> . . . you were a man/woman?
> . . . you were older/younger?
> . . . the weather was warmer/colder?
> . . . someone offered you a free trip to the North Pole?

So + Adjective/Such + Noun (pp. 105–108)

So . . . that and *such . . . that* are used to make clauses of result. *So* is used with adjectives (including *much* and *many*) and adverbs:

> He's so busy (that) he doesn't have time for his friends.
> She ate so much candy (that) she got sick.
> It rained so hard (that) we couldn't go outside.

Such is used with nouns:

> It was such a dangerous job (that) I was afraid to do it.
> She's such a friendly person (that) everyone likes her.

It is not necessary to say *that* in any of these sentences.

Have students combine sentences using *so* + adjective (*that*):

> That dog is stupid. You can't teach him anything.
> That dog is so stupid (that) you can't teach him anything.

> He's busy. He can't leave the office.
> His writing is bad. You can't read it.
> The radio is very loud. We can't talk.
> She's ill. She can't get out of bed.
> The bed is very hard. She can't sleep in it.
> This coffee is very hot. We can't drink it.
> This food is bad. We can't eat it.
> That dress is very small. She can't wear it.
> Those gloves are old. She can't use them any more.

Have students combine sentences using *such* + noun (*that*):

> It was a terrible meal. We couldn't eat it.
> It was such a terrible meal (that) we couldn't eat it.

> She had a bad headache. She couldn't do her homework.
> He had poor eyesight. He couldn't see a thing.
> He spoke with a heavy accent. We couldn't understand him.
> The car was in bad condition. They couldn't drive it.
> It was a hot day. They couldn't work.
> It was a cold night. She couldn't sleep.
> It was a long book. She couldn't finish it.
> It was a difficult question. He couldn't answer it.
> It was a heavy package. We couldn't lift it.

The -self Pronouns (p. 108)

These are: *myself, yourself, himself, herself, itself, ourselves, yourselves,* and *themselves.*

Used as **reflexive pronouns**:

The *-self* pronouns are used as objects of a verb when the subject and object of the verb are the same person:

> She's making herself a new dress.
> They always enjoy themselves at parties.

Used as **emphasizing pronouns**:

The *-self* pronouns can be used to emphasize a noun or pronoun:

> He repaired the car himself.
> I myself will teach you how to dance.

Used **after prepositions**:

The *-self* pronouns are also used after prepositions when the subject of the verb and the object of the preposition are the same person:

> She never talks about herself.
> He looked at himself in the mirror.

Write the *-self* pronouns on the chalkboard:

Singular		Plural	
me	myself	we	ourselves
you	yourself	you	yourselves
he	himself	they	themselves
she	herself		
it	itself		

Start a substitution drill using *-self* pronouns:

Teacher:	I enjoyed myself at the party. They.
Student:	They enjoyed themselves at the party.

Introduce other verbs that can be used with *-self* pronouns: *introduce, look at, hurt, take care of.*

CHAPTER 6

▶Answers

Reading 1 (p. 102)
Answers may vary.

1. Sam and Mabel wish they lived on a farm.
2. If they had a farm, they could raise animals and produce their own food.
3. Linda could have her own horse, and Jimmy could go hunting and fishing with his father.
4. Jimmy and Linda wouldn't be able to finish college and they would miss their friends.
5. Life in the country is hard work, but it's peaceful and quiet.

Reading 2 (p. 102)
Answers may vary.

1. Elmer and Sarah have a difficult life on their farm, but they are used to it.
2. In 1989 their house burned down. This year they have lost most of their corn and wheat crops due to bad weather. Last month, Nancy Paine crashed into their barn.
3. Sarah thinks it would be better if they moved to the city.
4. Elmer could get a job working in his brother's supermarket.
5. Sarah could open a bakery.
6. Answers will vary. I think that Elmer and Sarah should stay on the farm, because they are used to it, and cities are big and crowded.

Practice (p. 102)
1. If he knew her address, he could send her a letter.
2. If they had money, they could go to a movie.
3. If we had a car, we could drive to the beach.
4. If he knew how to swim, he could go in the water.
5. If I had my watch, I could tell you the time.
6. If she lived near her job, she could walk to work.
7. If he owned property, he could get a loan from the bank.
8. If we had their telephone number, we could call them.

Practice 1 (p. 104)
1. If he wanted to be a doctor, he would study medicine.
2. If she loved him, she would marry him.
3. If they were in a hurry, they would take a taxi.
4. If we were hungry, we would eat now.
5. If this book were interesting, I would finish reading it.
6. If he studied, he would pass the test.
7. If she respected him, she would take his advice.
8. If they practiced, they would improve.
9. If I liked them, I would help them.

Practice 2 (p. 104)
1. I wish he exercised more.
2. I wish she liked classical music.
3. I wish they had a car.
4. I wish I had more free time.
5. I wish we went out more often.
6. I wish he helped us more.
7. I wish she wrote more letters.
8. I wish they understood.
9. I wish I knew the answer.

Practice 3 (p. 104)
1. I wish she didn't talk so much.
2. I wish he didn't work so slowly.
3. I wish they didn't spend so much money.
4. I wish you didn't drive so fast.
5. I wish we didn't make so many mistakes.
6. I wish he didn't watch so much television.
7. I wish I didn't get tired so easily.
8. I wish you didn't eat so many pastries.
9. I wish she didn't waste so much time.

Reading (p. 106)
Answers may vary.

1. Ula Hackey thought that Barney had such an interesting personality that he would make a good actor.
2. She wanted Barney to play the part of a taxi driver.
3. Barney was so excited that he couldn't sleep at night.
4. He memorized his part in less than a week.
5. Miss Hackey was so pleased with his progress that she decided to leave for Hollywood right away and take Barney with her.
6. Everyone was uncomfortable because it was such a hot day.
7. The director didn't like Barney because he wasn't a professional actor. He yelled at Barney several times.
8. He was so nervous that he could hardly talk. He was so discouraged that he felt like quitting.
9. She came over and tried to cheer him up.

Practice (p. 106)
1. Linda is so tired that she can't finish her homework.
2. Mr. Bascomb is so busy that he can't leave the office.
3. This box is so heavy that I can't lift it.
4. Mr. Twaddle is so short that he can't reach the window.
5. He's so poor that he can't buy a new pair of shoes.
6. His bed is so uncomfortable that he can't sleep in it.
7. The bus is so crowded that Mrs. Golo can't find a seat.
8. She's so boring that I can't listen to her.

Practice (p. 108)

1. She has such a nice personality that everyone likes her.
2. We were having such a pleasant talk that I didn't want to leave.
3. Dr. Pasto is such an intelligent man that everyone listens to him.
4. He's had such an exciting life that he could write a book about it.
5. Anne has such a good voice that she could be a professional singer.
6. She lives in such a small apartment that she can't have visitors.
7. Mr. Bascomb is such a powerful man that everyone is afraid of him.
8. He's such a busy man that he doesn't have time for his family.

Written Exercise (p. 108)

1. I bought __myself__ a new pair of shoes.
2. She taught __herself__ to play the guitar.
3. We enjoyed __ourselves__ at the party.
4. He made __himself__ a sandwich.
5. You can all take care of __yourselves__.
6. She looked at __herself__ in the mirror.
7. He didn't recognize __himself__ after he got a haircut.
8. They always talk about __themselves__.

Story Questions (p. 111)

Answers may vary.

1. Fred Farmer has been looking for a job for several months, but he hasn't been able to find anything that suits his personality.
2. He called on Dr. Pasto, a man everyone goes to when they are having problems.
3. He doesn't have any training, and there aren't any jobs for people without skills.
4. He spends most of his time at the park teaching kids how to play baseball.
5. They have nothing to do, so they become juvenile delinquents.
6. Fred tries to look after Marty because Marty reminds Fred of himself when he was a boy. Also, Marty's father died a few years ago, and Marty misses him.
7. He was in Dr. Pasto's backyard taking apples from his tree.
8. He gets along with boys like Marty because they have fun together.
9. He could start a club for boys.
10. He can't do it by himself because it's a big job, and it takes a lot of money to start a boys' club. Fred is broke.
11. Because Otis Jackson is concerned about the youth in their town, and if he wins the election for mayor, he could help Fred get the money for the boys' club.
12. Answers will vary.

Pair Work (p. 111)

Answers will vary.

Written Exercise (p. 112)

1. Our friends live so far away (that) we can't see them very often.
2. My sister talks so fast (that) no one can understand her.
3. Mr. Bascomb meets so many people (that) he can't remember all their names.
4. He works so much (that) he doesn't have time for his family.
5. He was so tired last night (that) he went to bed right after dinner.
6. He worries so much (that) he can't sleep at night.
7. It was raining so hard yesterday (that) we couldn't go outside.
8. We ate so much candy (that) we got sick.
9. Barney tells so many stories (that) I can't remember them all.
10. He enjoys acting so much (that) he doesn't want to drive a taxi anymore.

Pair Work (p. 112)

1. A: Did Peter repair his car?
   B: Yes, he repaired it himself.
2. A: Did Barbara and Tino paint their house?
   B: Yes, they painted it themselves.
3. A: Did Nancy fix her TV set?
   B: Yes, she fixed it herself.
4. A: Did Jimmy plan the party?
   B: Yes, he planned it himself.
5. A: Did you make the cake?
   B: Yes, I made it myself.
6. A: Did the women pay for their vacation?
   B: Yes, they paid for it themselves.
7. A: Did Mr. Bascomb write that speech?
   B: Yes, he wrote it himself.
8. A: Did Anne carry those boxes?
   B: Yes, she carried them herself.
9. A: Did the boys plant the apple tree?
   B: Yes, they planted it themselves.
10. A: Did you cut your hair?
    B: Yes, I cut it myself.

Free Response (p. 113)

Answers will vary.

Group Work (p. 113)

Answers will vary.

"Work" Questions (p. 114)

Answers will vary.

Talking about Places to Live, Role Play, Talking about Juvenile Delinquency, and Group Work (p. 115)

Answers will vary.

WORKBOOK EXERCISES

▶**ANSWERS**

Exercise 1 (p. 49)
1. If they painted their house, it would look much better.
2. If she took the bus to work, she would save money.
3. If I told you the truth, you wouldn't believe me.
4. If you planned ahead, you wouldn't have any problems.
5. If you were nice to people, they would be nice to you.
6. If she joined the Student Club, she would make a lot of friends.
7. If he went to the dance, he would have a good time.
8. If I sold my car, I wouldn't have any transportation.
9. If you exercised more, you would feel better.
10. If you took care of yourself, you wouldn't get sick.

Exercise 2 (p. 50)
Answers will vary.

Exercise 3 (p. 50)
Answers will vary.

Exercise 4 (p. 50)
Answers will vary.

Exercise 5 (p. 51)
1. If I were you, I'd follow the doctor's advice.
2. If I were you, I'd stop smoking.
3. If I were you, I'd go to bed earlier.
4. If I were you, I'd get more exercise.
5. If I were you, I'd eat more vegetables.
6. If I were you, I'd take up a sport.
7. If I were you, I'd go out more often.
8. If I were you, I'd take dancing lessons.
9. If I were you, I'd get some new shoes.
10. If I were you, I'd wear a coat and tie.

Exercise 6 (p. 51)
1. I hurt _myself_ in a basketball game last weekend.
2. It's too bad you can't see _yourself_ in the mirror, Miss Jones.
3. Gloria promised _herself_ that she would go out more often.
4. Why don't you guys get _yourselves_ some new clothes?
5. I sometimes ask _myself_ the same question.
6. People always enjoy _themselves_ at my parties.
7. I want all of you to make _yourselves_ at home.
8. Can we help _ourselves_ to some lemonade and cookies?
9. Tino is pouring _himself_ a cup of coffee.
10. His parents introduced _themselves_ to me a few minutes ago.

Exercise 7 (p. 52)
Answers may vary.
1. She was so tired that she fell asleep on the bus.
2. The cake was so good that he ate all of it.
3. She was so proud of her boyfriend that she gave him a kiss.
4. The movie was so sad that everyone cried.
5. Her shoes were so uncomfortable that she took them off.
6. The coffee was so hot that he couldn't drink it.
7. His speech was so boring that everyone fell asleep.
8. She was so heavy that she broke the chair.

Exercise 8 (p. 53)
Answers may vary.
1. It's such an interesting book that he can't put it down.
2. He's such a good artist that everyone wants to buy his paintings.
3. She's such a beautiful woman that everyone looks at her.
4. It's such a hard bed that he can't sleep in it.
5. He's such a mean dog that everyone is afraid of him.
6. It's such a heavy suitcase that she can't lift it.
7. She's such a bad cook that nobody eats her food.
8. He's such a big man that he can't get in the car.

Exercise 9 (p. 54)
Answers will vary.

Exercise 10 (p. 54)
1. Jane doesn't have much money, but she dresses like she had a lot of money.
2. She isn't my girlfriend, but she acts like she were my girlfriend.
3. You don't know everything, but sometimes you talk like you knew everything.
4. You say you're happy, but you don't look like you were happy.
5. The Hambys aren't rich, but they spend money like they were rich.
6. Mr. Hamby isn't my boss, but sometimes he acts like he were my boss.
7. He doesn't have an important job, but he talks like he had an important job.
8. I'm not crazy, so don't look at me like I were crazy.
9. Anne isn't a child, but sometimes Johnnie talks to her like she were a child.
10. That woman doesn't know me, so why does she smile at me like she knew me?

Exercise 11 (p. 55)

1. A few weeks ago, we met some Brazilian tourists at a party.
2. They were from São Paulo, which is in southern Brazil.
3. They didn't speak much English, but we managed to communicate with them.
4. It was their first time in America, and they wanted to see everything.
5. We took them to Disneyland, Sea World, and Universal Studios.
6. They asked us to visit them in São Paulo, and we accepted their invitation.
7. If all goes well, we'll see our new friends next spring.
8. Oh, did you hear about the new movie that's playing at the Rex Theater?
9. It's a musical comedy starring Constance Cooney.
10. My favorite movie, *The Bicycle Thief,* was made in Italy.
11. I studied film at the University of California in Los Angeles.
12. You didn't know that, did you?

Exercise 12 (p. 56)
Composition

▶PRELIMINARY ORAL WORK

Gerunds (pp. 120–122)

Gerunds after expressions:
The gerund is used after the expressions *be used to* and *get used to:*

> She's used to working hard.
> He's used to getting up early.
> You'll get used to wearing glasses.
> They'll get used to taking the bus.

Used to:

Teacher:	I get up early every morning. I'm used to getting up early. I take the bus every day. I'm used to taking the bus. Tell me something you didn't like in the beginning but are now used to doing.
Student:	I'm used to washing the dishes.

Gerunds after prepositions:
When a verb follows an adjective + preposition the gerund form must be used:

> He's tired of working at the bank.
> I'm excited about going to France.

Ask students questions using adjective + preposition:

Teacher:	I'm good at repairing things. What are you good at doing?
Student:	I'm good at writing letters.

Bring in other adjective + preposition phrases: *afraid of, interested in, responsible for, tired of,* etc.

Gerunds after Prepositions (pp. 123–126)

The gerund form is used after a verb + preposition:

> She dreams about getting married.
> He apologized for breaking the vase.

Ask students questions using a verb + preposition:

Teacher:	I look forward to reading this letter from my sister. What do you look forward to doing?
Student:	I look forward to seeing my girl-friend.

Bring in other verb + preposition phrases: *feel like, think about, believe in, don't believe in, object to, dream of,* etc.

The gerund form is often used after the words *before* and *after:*

> She brushed her teeth before she went to bed.
> She brushed her teeth before going to bed.

> He called his wife after he left the office.
> He called his wife after leaving the office.

We also use the gerund form after the words *for, by, without,* and *while:*

> She criticized him for coming home late.
> He made a lot of money by working overtime.
> You can learn to type without taking lessons.
> He complained about the cold weather while refusing to wear a coat.

CHAPTER 7

▶ANSWERS

Reading (p. 120)
Answers may vary.

1. Mr. Fix used to be a real estate agent.
2. He got rich by selling worthless farmland to people from the city who didn't know what they were buying.
3. He used the money he got from selling farmland to buy an old apartment building in Wickam City.
4. He wanted the tenants to leave the building so he could make a few minor improvements and then charge high rents.
5. He chose to get rid of them by making life miserable for everyone in the building. He drew up a long list of unnecessary regulations and insisted that everyone obey him. At times he even cut off the electricity.
6. When the tenants complained, Mr. Fix always defended his actions and told the tenants to leave if they weren't happy.
7. He almost succeeded in driving everyone out of the building, but he didn't count on the opposition he got from one of his tenants, an old lady named Olive Grove.

Practice (p. 120)
Answers will vary.

Practice (p. 122)
1. My sister is sorry for causing so much trouble.
2. She is tired of working late.
3. Jimmy is interested in studying medicine.
4. He is good at repairing things.
5. Barbara is capable of running a mile in five minutes.
6. We are responsible for taking out the trash.
7. I am ashamed of driving that old car.
8. Jenny and Mary are fond of eating ice cream.
9. They are excited about going to the movies.

Reading (p. 124)
Answers may vary.

1. Olive Grove went back to the Bedford Arms and called a meeting of all the tenants who were still living in the building.
2. She told them there would be a trial, and they would have the opportunity to settle their differences with Mr. Fix once and for all.
3. Yes, the tenants drew up a petition listing their complaints.
4. They objected to Mr. Fix raising the rent without making the necessary improvements, forcing people out of their apartments for not obeying the new rules, "saving energy" by cutting off the electricity, and making money on property while doing nothing to maintain it.
5. They took their petition to Mr. Case.
6. Mr. Duke was Mr. Fix's lawyer.
7. Yes, he made several good points in defense of his client.
8. Justin Case seemed to have the strongest arguments.

Practice (p. 124)
1. The tenants criticized Mr. Fix for raising the rent.
2. Mr. Fix criticized his tenants for not obeying the rules.
3. We criticized our neighbors for playing loud music.
4. Mr. Farley criticized his wife for spending too much money.
5. Mrs. Farley criticized her husband for not taking out the trash.
6. The students criticized their teacher for giving them too much homework.
7. The teacher criticized the students for not doing their homework.
8. Mr. Bascomb criticized his employees for coming to work late.

Dialogue Questions (p. 125)
Answers will vary.

1. The court found Mr. Fix guilty of violating his tenants' right to fair housing.
2. Mr. Fix broke the law by forcing people out of their apartments to benefit himself.
3. The judge ordered Mr. Fix to pay court costs for both sides, make all necessary improvements in Bedford Arms, maintain his property according to the building code, not raise the rent more than 5 percent a year, and respect the rights of his tenants.
4. Answers will vary. I think the judge was fair with Mr. Fix.
5. If Mr. Fix doesn't obey the judge's order, the court will fine him $5,000.
6. Mr. Fix was apologetic, he says, because he didn't realize how badly he was treating the tenants.
7. Answers will vary. No, I don't think he will be a good landlord, because he knew all along that he was being mean and unfair.

Practice (p. 126)
1. Olive is planning on celebrating.
2. We apologize for making so much noise.
3. I insist on seeing your brother.
4. He is against asking for help.
5. He believes in being independent.
6. Mr. Hamby plans on selling his house.
7. He's looking forward to living in Spain.
8. Anne is thinking about leaving her job.

9. She objects to taking orders from Mr. Bascomb.
10. He believes in working hard.
11. Mabel complains about getting up early.
12. She puts off doing the housework.

Story Questions (p. 128)
Answers may vary.

1. The other day Barbara was walking in the park when she saw Anne Jones sitting by herself on a bench.
2. Anne was crying because of a dream she had last night.
3. The strange man was a talent scout for Delta Music.
4. He asked Anne to go with him for an audition.
5. Her first song was a surprise success and sold a million copies.
6. Her face was on the cover of *Time* magazine.
7. The famous director wanted Anne to star in a movie.
8. An Arabian oil sheikh asked Anne to marry him.
9. She was crying because she woke up from the beautiful dream.
10. Answers may vary. Anne's dream tells us that she is easily swept away by fantasies.

Written Exercise (p. 128)
1. They decided _to leave_ at seven o'clock.
2. You should call before _going_ over there.
3. She plans _to visit_ her mother.
4. I'm thinking about _selling_ my camera.
5. We need the lamp for _reading_ .
6. He hopes _to study_ medicine.
7. She got to be a good tennis player by _practicing_ .
8. I was glad I had a chance _to meet_ Dr. Pasto.
9. Do you mind _waiting_ outside?
10. It's important for us _to be_ patient.
11. Don't forget _to call_ me.
12. I look forward to _seeing_ you again.

Free Response (p. 128)
Answers will vary.

Pair Work (p. 129)
Answers will vary.

1. A: Excuse me. How can I get to Sunset Park from here?
   B: Go one and a half blocks down Central Avenue to Willow Street. Turn right on Willow. Go two blocks. You'll see it on the corner of Hill and Willow.
2. A: Excuse me. How can I get to the gas station from here?
   B: Go one block down Dixon to Gage Avenue. Turn right on Gage and go almost two blocks. You'll see it on the left. It's next to Ben's Shoe Repair.

3. A: Excuse me. How can I get to the Holiday Hotel from here?
   B: Go two blocks down Hill Street to Dixon Avenue. Turn right on Dixon. You'll see it on the right, on the corner of Dixon and Gage.
4. A: Excuse me. How can I get to Gold's Department Store from here?
   B: Go up Dixon to Hill Street. Turn left on Hill. Go a block and a half. You'll see it on the left.
5. A: Excuse me. How can I get to Marino Restaurant from here?
   B: Go two blocks on Hill Street to Willow Street. Turn left on Willow. You'll see the Marino Restaurant on the left, on the corner of Willow and Central.
6. A: Excuse me. How can I get to Larry's Garage from here?
   B: Go two blocks on Central Avenue to Willow Street. Turn right. Larry's Garage is on the corner of Willow and Gage.
7. A: Excuse me. How can I get to the public library from here?
   B: Go one block to Oak and turn left on Oak. Go two blocks to Hill Street. Turn right on Hill Street. Go one block. It'll be on your left.
8. A: Excuse me. How can I get to the Rose Cafe from here?
   B: Go down Gage, take your first right onto Oak Street. Go one block. The Rose Cafe is on the left, on the corner of Oak and Central.

Class Activity (p. 130)
Answers will vary.

1. John is arriving at a party.
2. He's giving flowers to the hostess.
3. She's putting the flowers in a vase.
4. She is introducing him to another guest.
5. The hostess is showing them the food.
6. John and the other guest are chatting.
7. Some of the guests are singing, and others are listening.
8. John is getting the other guest's phone number.
9. John is leaving the party.

Written Exercise (p. 130)
2. These are for you.
3. They're beautiful.
4. John, this is Mary.
5. Help yourselves.
6. This is delicious.
7. Do you know that song?
8. Could I have your phone number?
9. Thank you for a wonderful evening.

Vocabulary Practice, Group Work 1, Group Work 2, Role Play, and Group Work 3 (p. 131)
Answers will vary.

"Dreams" Questions (p. 132)

Answers may vary.

1. Anne appears to be a rather timid, plain-looking woman with little ambition.
2. Anne sees herself as a popular, talented singer. Her Shadow is the talented, outgoing side of her that appears in her dreams.
3. Anne is a bored secretary working in a small-town bank. She dislikes her job because it offers very little opportunity for self-expression. She knows she could be getting much more out of life and feels frustrated.
4. Her dream is trying to satisfy her need to be successful and admired.
5. Dreams are difficult to understand because they are a product of the subconscious mind.
6. Dreams reveal our hidden feelings and desires and help us to see ourselves as we really are.

Free Response (p. 132)

Answers will vary.

Class Activity

1. Barney is dreaming that he is riding in a convertible with Ula Hackey. Barney is a big Hollywood producer, and Ula Hackey is crazy about him. Everywhere they go, people smile and wave to them.

2. Gladys is dreaming that she is the queen of England. She lives in Buckingham Palace and can have anything she wants. She gives fancy parties for her friends and they say, "Long live the Queen!"
3. Mr. Bascomb is dreaming that he is the president of the United States. He is the most powerful man in the world. He makes wise decisions and gives excellent speeches. All the American people love him.
4. Mr. Fix is dreaming that he is in prison. He is sitting alone in a cold, dark cell. There is nothing to do and no one to talk to. The food is so bad that the rats won't eat it. He is having a nightmare!

Listening Practice and Pair Work (p. 133)

Answers will vary.

Talking about the Legal System, Talking about Renting Apartments, Role Play, and Composition (p. 134)

Answers will vary.

WORKBOOK EXERCISES

▶ANSWERS

Exercise 1 (p. 59)
1. He's sorry about breaking Mrs. Golo's window.
2. She's good at playing tennis.
3. She's interested in learning to dance.
4. He's fond of playing the piano.
5. She's tired of waiting for the bus.
6. She's excited about getting a letter from France.
7. He's concerned with making more money.
8. She's upset about burning the steak.

Exercise 2 (p. 60)
Answers will vary.

Exercise 3 (p. 60)
Answers will vary.

Exercise 4 (p. 61)
1. She dreams of becoming a singer.
2. He plans on buying a used car.
3. He worries about finding a job.
4. He objects to wearing a tie.
5. He believes in eating well.
6. She admits to being a bad cook.
7. She insists on paying the bill.
8. He looks forward to having his own business.

Exercise 5 (p. 62)
Answers will vary.

Exercise 6 (p. 62)
1. I invited her to have lunch with me.
2. We agreed to meet at the Martinoli Restaurant.
3. She left her house without taking an umbrella.
4. She didn't mind walking in the rain.
5. She arrived a few minutes late, but I was glad to see her.
6. We had to wait twenty minutes for the waiter to bring the menu.
7. She criticized him for taking so long.
8. I asked her to order something inexpensive.
9. She felt like having a big steak.
10. She believes in eating well.

Exercise 7 (p. 63)
1. He left the house without eating breakfast.
2. She bought the dress without trying it on.
3. He worked all afternoon without taking a rest.
4. She spent all the money without telling her husband.
5. It rained for three days without stopping.
6. He repaired the car without getting his hands dirty.
7. He cooked dinner without making a mess.
8. We waited in line for two hours without complaining.
9. They got married without telling anyone.
10. I passed the exam without studying for it.
11. She entered the room without making a sound.

Exercise 8 (p. 64)
1. The men want to work only twenty hours a week, but that doesn't make sense.
2. They can't buy anything because they are broke.
3. I'm not a very fast worker, but I'll do my best.
4. You should take your time in the beginning.
5. It doesn't look like we'll ever get through all this work.
6. I have to take back the books I borrowed last week.
7. Why don't you get rid of those old magazines?
8. Everyone looks up to Dr. Pasto.
9. Even when things go wrong, he never loses his temper.
10. This is the first time I've ever traveled by plane, and I'm a little on edge.
11. She'll probably turn up at the last minute.
12. Are you going to dress up for the party tomorrow?

Exercise 9 (p. 64)
Answers will vary.

Exercise 10 (p. 65)
1. about
2. for
3. of
4. from
5. of
6. for
7. to
8. with
9. in
10. at
11. between

Exercise 11 (p. 65)
Answers will vary.

Exercise 12 (p. 65)
Answers will vary.

Exercise 13 (p. 66)
Answers will vary.

Exercise 14 (p. 66)
Answers will vary.

CHAPTER 8

▶**ANSWERS**

Story Questions (p. 141)
Answers may vary.

1. Sam and Jimmy went fishing at Bear Lake.
2. When they arrived, they saw a beautiful sunrise over the lake.
3. Bear Lake got its name because a long time ago, when Jimmy's grandfather was a boy, there were bears living in that forest.
4. The best place to catch fish is the north end of the lake.
5. The fish Jimmy caught was the biggest one that he'd ever seen. It was six pounds.
6. Sam put the fish in the back of the boat, and a bear took it out and ate it.
7. When Sam saw the bear, he started the motor, and the boat began to speed out of the shadow.
8. He meant that they came close to having big problems.
9. Answers will vary. Sam and Jimmy learned that there still are bears around the lake.
10. Answers will vary. I would go fishing at Bear Lake because I'd like to see a bear.
11. Answers will vary.
12. Answers will vary.

Group Work (p. 141)
Answers will vary.

Practice (p. 141)
1. He's so ambitious (that) he'll do anything to succeed.
2. She's so lazy (that) she won't clean the floor.
3. It's such an unpleasant job (that) nobody wants to do it.
4. I was so worried last night (that) I couldn't sleep.
5. You made such a loud noise this morning (that) everyone woke up.
6. She's such a dangerous driver (that) it's unsafe to go anywhere with her.
7. Your car is so small (that) you can park it anywhere.
8. He's such a mysterious man (that) nobody knows anything about him.
9. She's such an interesting woman (that) everyone wants to meet her.
10. They're so talented (that) you've got to admire them.

Written Exercise (p. 141)
1. victory   defeat
2. fail   succeed
3. private   public
4. above   below
5. interesting   boring
6. strength   weakness
7. oppose   support
8. nervous   relaxed
9. most   least
10. winner   loser
11. valuable   worthless
12. familiar   strange

Pair Work (p. 142)
Answers will vary.

1. A: Otis Jackson and Mr. Bascomb are both good candidates for mayor.
   B: I think Otis is a better candidate.
   A: Why?
   B: Because he supports keeping City Park.
   A: You're right. *or* I disagree. I think Mr. Bascomb is better because we need more jobs.
2. A: Politicians and used-car dealers are both dishonest.
   B: I think used-car dealers are more dishonest.
   A: Why?
   B: Because they have to sell lots of bad cars to lots of unsuspecting people every day!
   A: You're right. *or* I disagree. I think politicians are more dishonest because they have to sell themselves to the public!
3. A: Sports and politics are both interesting.
   B: I think politics are more interesting.
   A: Why?
   B: Because politics affect every part of our lives.
   A: I agree. *or* I disagree. I think sports are more interesting because they involve real people in an honest competition.
4. A: Money and friendship are both important.
   B: I think friendship is more important.
   A: Why?
   B: Because we can't live without friends.
   A: I agree. *or* I disagree. I think money is more important because we really can't live without money.
5. A: Rock music and jazz are both popular.
   B: I think jazz is more popular.
   A: Why?
   B: Because lots of people listen to jazz.
   A: I agree. *or* I disagree. I think rock is more popular because every year more rock CDs are sold than jazz CDs.
6. A: Boxing and bullfighting are both dangerous sports.
   B: I think boxing is more dangerous.
   A: Why?
   B: Because in boxing you might have hidden injuries that get worse over time.
   A: I agree. *or* I disagree. I think bullfighting is more dangerous because a bull could easily kill you.

7. A: Driving a public bus and driving a taxi are both hard jobs.
   B: I think driving a public bus is harder.
   A: Why?
   B: Because a bus is much bigger than a taxi.
   A: I agree. *or* I disagree. I think driving a taxi is harder because taxi drivers are stuck in their cab with a person who might be crazy!

8. A: English and Spanish are both important languages.
   B: I think English is more important.
   A: Why?
   B: Because it's the international language.
   A: I agree. *or* I disagree. I think Spanish is more important because lots of people speak Spanish as their first language, but not enough people study it as a foreign language.

9. A: Hawaii and Alaska are both good places for vacations.
   B: I think Alaska is a better place for vacations.
   A: Why?
   B: Because it is so interesting.
   A: I agree. *or* I disagree. I think Hawaii is a better place for vacations because you can swim and go to the beach there.

Group Work (p. 142)
Answers will vary.

Written Exercise (p. 142)
1. If you take lessons, you __will be able to__ play the guitar in a few months.
2. I __would rather__ play the piano than play the guitar.
3. Your car is running pretty well, so you __won't have to__ repair it.
4. He works on Saturday, so he __won't be able to__ see the football game.
5. She likes to swim, but she __would rather__ play tennis.
6. If she wants to be a good tennis player, she __will have to__ practice.
7. If they close the park, we __won't be able to__ have any more picnics.
8. You'd better take your umbrella. It __might__ rain.
9. We have plenty of food at home, so we __won't have to__ go to the market.
10. If my brother becomes a doctor, he __will be able to__ help sick people.
11. If he wants to be a doctor, he __will have to__ study hard.
12. Don't forget your dictionary. You __might__ need it.

Pair Work (p. 144)
1. A: What's wrong with Anne?
   B: She's nervous because Mr. Bascomb is yelling at her.

A: She gets nervous easily, doesn't she?
B: I don't know. How would you feel if your boss yelled at you?
A: I guess I'd be nervous, too.

2. A: What's wrong with Johnnie?
   B: He's upset because there's a fly in his soup.
   A: He gets upset easily, doesn't he?
   B: I don't know. How would you feel if you had a fly in your soup?
   A: I guess I'd be upset, too.

3. A: What's wrong with Gladys?
   B: She's depressed because nobody asked her to dance.
   A: She gets depressed easily, doesn't she?
   B: I don't know. How would you feel if nobody asked you to dance?
   A: I guess I'd be depressed, too.

4. A: What's wrong with Mr. Farley?
   B: He's worried because he has lots of bills.
   A: He gets worried easily, doesn't he?
   B: I don't know. How would you feel if you had lots of bills?
   A: I guess I'd be worried, too.

5. A: What's wrong with Ed?
   B: He's bored because he doesn't have anything to do.
   A: He gets bored easily, doesn't he?
   B: I don't know. How would you feel if you didn't have anything to do?
   A: I guess I'd be bored, too.

6. A: What's wrong with Gladys?
   B: She's scared because she saw a strange man.
   A: She gets scared easily, doesn't she?
   B: I don't know. How would you feel if you saw a strange man?
   A: I guess I'd be scared, too.

Group Work (p. 144)
Answers will vary.

Pair Work (p. 145)
Answers will vary.

Written Exercise 1 (p. 145)
1. Maria painted the kitchen __herself__.
2. The children can take care of __themselves__.
3. I like to think of __myself__ as a good person.
4. You're smart people; you can decide for __yourselves__.
5. Mr. Grubb lives by __himself__ in a small apartment.
6. I looked at __myself__ in the mirror.
7. We helped __ourselves__ to some cake and ice cream.
8. You may have a big appetite, but you could never eat all that food by __yourself__.

Written Exercise 2 (p. 145)
1. We're excited __about__ meeting your family.
2. They plan __on__ staying here __for__ a week.

3. Anne is interested _in_ becoming a professional singer.
4. She dreams _of_ going _to_ Hollywood.
5. Johnnie is thinking _about_ buying a car.
6. He's tired _of_ taking the bus _to_ work.
7. Barbara believes _in_ getting a lot of exercise.

Practice (p. 148)

1. I wish she would talk to Peter.
2. I wish they would come and see us.
3. I wish we could call them at work.
4. I wish she would tell us what happened.
5. I wish I could do something about it.
6. I wish they would do their part.
7. I wish we could count on them.
8. I wish he could relax and enjoy himself.
9. I wish he would forget the past.

Written Exercise (p. 148)

Answers will vary.

Practice 1 (p. 151)

1. Where is the library?
2. How long will you be at the library?
3. Who does that book belong to?
4. Why didn't he go to the party?
5. When is the final exam?
6. How often do they play tennis?
7. Who usually wins?
8. How long has she been playing tennis?
9. Which dress did she buy?
10. Where does she like to shop?
11. How long did he sleep last night?
12. What did he have for breakfast this morning?

Practice 2 (p. 151)

1. He promised he would repair the garage door.
2. She promised she would make spaghetti for dinner.
3. They promised they would come to the party.
4. She promised she would call me.
5. You promised you would introduce him to me.
6. They promised they would wait for us.
7. He promised he would return the dictionary.
8. She promised she would attend the meeting.

"Six Deadly Career Sins You Can Avoid"
Questions (p. 152)

Answers will vary.

Free Response (p. 154)

Answers will vary.

Test (p. 155)

1. C	14. A	27. A	39. A
2. D	15. C	28. D	40. B
3. B	16. A	29. C	41. D
4. A	17. C	30. B	42. B
5. D	18. D	31. B	43. D
6. B	19. B	32. C	44. A
7. A	20. C	33. D	45. C
8. B	21. A	34. D	46. A
9. C	22. D	35. C	47. D
10. C	23. B	36. A	48. D
11. A	24. D	37. B	49. B
12. D	25. A	38. C	50. C
13. B	26. C		

WORKBOOK EXERCISES

▶ ANSWERS

Exercise 1 (pp. 69–70)

Linda:	Albert, when was the last time we had a party?
Albert:	I don't know. It's been a long time.
Linda:	I think we <u>should</u> have a party and invite all our friends.
Albert:	Good idea. When <u>would</u> you like to have it?
Linda:	Friday night. We <u>can</u> have the party at my house.
Albert:	I'm sorry. I <u>can't</u> make it Friday night. How about Saturday night?
Linda:	That's fine with me. Do you think we <u>should</u> have food at the party?
Albert:	Of course. We <u>can't</u> have a party without food.
Linda:	I knew you <u>would</u> say that. Okay, we <u>will</u> have some potato chips and punch.
Albert:	. . . and sandwiches and cake and ice cream and . . .
Linda:	Albert, you <u>must</u> be joking. We <u>can't</u> afford to buy all that food. It's too expensive.
Albert:	Don't worry. We <u>will</u> ask everyone to bring a dollar. That way you and I <u>won't</u> have to pay for everything.
Linda:	Well, that <u>might</u> be a good idea. But it <u>might</u> also be a mistake.
Albert:	Why?
Linda:	Some people <u>may</u> not want to come if they have to bring money.
Albert:	That's crazy. If they <u>can't</u> help us pay for the food, they <u>shouldn't</u> come.
Linda:	I suppose you're right. But it takes more than food to have a good party. We need some music. Do you know anyone who <u>can</u> play the guitar?
Albert:	Sure. There's Benny Barnes. He plays the guitar better than anyone. <u>Should</u> we invite Benny?
Linda:	No, please, not Benny. He <u>may</u> be a good guitar player, but he <u>always</u> makes a fool of himself at parties. He <u>might</u> do something crazy.
Albert:	Yeah, I remember the last time when he started dancing on top of the dining table. We <u>couldn't</u> get him off. He just kept <u>dancing</u>.
Linda:	I hope nothing like that happens Saturday night.
Albert:	Don't worry. We're going to have a nice little party. Everything <u>will</u> be fine.

Exercise 2 (p. 70)

Answers may vary.

Exercise 3 (p. 71)

Answers may vary.

1. smaller
2. faster
3. longer
4. more expensive
5. stronger
6. better
7. harder
8. sooner
9. closer
10. more careful

Exercise 4 (p. 71)

1. "If I <u>had</u> a girlfriend, I <u>wouldn't</u> be so lonely."
2. "If I <u>didn't eat</u> so much, I <u>wouldn't</u> be so fat."
3. "If I <u>studied,</u> I <u>would get</u> better grades."
4. "If I <u>didn't drink</u> so much coffee, I <u>wouldn't have</u> trouble sleeping."
5. "If people <u>ate</u> more vegetables, they <u>would be</u> healthier."
6. "If I <u>had</u> a lot of money, I <u>would travel</u> around the world."
7. "If I <u>had</u> something to do, I <u>wouldn't be</u> so bored."
8. "If people <u>got</u> more exercise, they <u>would live</u> longer."
9. "If more people <u>read</u> my books, I <u>would be</u> very happy."

Exercise 5 (p. 72)

1. Sandy walks to work every morning.
2. Does she still work at the same place?
3. I haven't talked to her recently.
4. I hope to see Sandy soon.
5. I like her very much.
6. She is probably at home this evening.
7. She listens to the radio all the time.
8. She likes rock music and also likes jazz.
9. Sandy used to play the piano very well.
10. Unfortunately, she doesn't play anymore.

Exercise 6 (p. 72)

Answers will vary.

Exercise 7 (p. 73)

1. He always complains about <u>doing</u> the housework, but he's never too tired <u>to play</u> tennis.
2. He learned how <u>to cook</u> by <u>watching</u> his girlfriend.
3. He plans on <u>asking</u> her <u>to marry</u> him.
4. He has decided <u>to study</u> medicine. He wants <u>to become</u> a doctor.
5. She seems <u>to like working</u> at the bank.
6. We're excited about <u>going</u> to New York this summer. Our uncle invited us <u>to stay</u> with him.

7. He's capable of <u>doing</u> almost anything, but he refuses <u>to work</u> very hard.
8. He allowed me <u>to use</u> his camera, and I promised <u>to take</u> good care of it.
9. Are you good at <u>making</u> things? I think it's fun <u>to work</u> with your hands.
10. Jimmy enjoys <u>repairing</u> cars, but he doesn't have enough experience <u>to get</u> a job as a mechanic.
11. We encouraged him <u>to study</u> hard when he was in high school. Now he's thinking about <u>going</u> to college.
12. He thanked us for <u>taking</u> an interest in him. He hopes <u>to help</u> others in the future.

Exercise 8 (p. 74)
1. Sandy wore a lot of makeup so people would notice her.
2. The boss gave her a raise in pay so she wouldn't quit her job.
3. She wrote her telephone number on his forehead so he wouldn't forget it.
4. She called home every week so her parents wouldn't worry about her.
5. They got her a used car so she would have some transportation.
6. Her brother fixed up the car so she wouldn't spend money on repairs.
7. She fed him a lot of potatoes so he would put on weight.
8. We gave her a ride to work so she wouldn't be late.
9. She wrote the boss a letter so he would know what was going on.
10. She put the letter on his desk so he would see it when he came in.

Exercise 9 (p. 75)
Dear Gloria,

I'm in Rio de Janeiro. I arrived here the day before yesterday. I'm staying at the Palace Hotel, which is very comfortable and right across the street from the beach. Rio is a beautiful city, with mountains, forests, tropical gardens, and miles of sandy beaches. It's also a very noisy city. There are a lot of traffic jams, and people are always honking their horns.

I've been pretty busy since I arrived. The first day I took a cable car to the top of Sugar Loaf, a huge rock that overlooks the entrance to Guanabara Bay. From the top of Sugar Loaf, you can read Rio like a map. I went up at sunset and saw the beautiful city lights below.

Yesterday I saw a samba parade near the center of town. There was a band playing percussion instruments and lots of dancers in exotic costumes. They came dressed as lords and ladies, pirates, clowns, and animals. There were hundreds of spectators on both sides of the street. Everyone was dancing, singing, and shouting with joy. It was fabulous.

Today is my last day in Rio. I'm going to do some shopping this morning, then I'm going to the beach. The weather is sunny and warm, so I'm sure there will be a lot of people on the beach. I'm having a wonderful time here and would like to come back again. I hope everything's fine with you.

See you soon,
Sandy

Exercise 10 (p. 76)
Composition